Make a Quantum Leap in Your Consciousness on the Road To Ascension

Dr. Richard A. Huntoon

authorHOUSE®

AuthorHouse™
1663 Liberty Drive
Bloomington, IN 47403
www.authorhouse.com
Phone: 1-800-839-8640

First published by AuthorHouse   11/11/2011

ISBN: 978-1-4634-1052-0 (ebk)
ISBN: 978-1-4634-1051-3 (sc)

Library of Congress Control Number: 2011909512

Printed in the United States of America

Any people depicted in stock imagery provided by Thinkstock are models, and such images are being used for illustrative purposes only. Certain stock imagery © Thinkstock.

This book is printed on acid-free paper.

Design and Layout by Dr. Richard A. Huntoon and Marketing Works, Inc.

This book is written for people who want to improve their physical, mental, emotional and spiritual health. The conscious adoption and use of this material by the reader may, temporarily, increase current life issues. This is a positive indication of change, and is expected when seeking transformative experiences. Nothing in the book is meant to diagnose or treat specific health conditions and all recommendations in the book are made after careful evaluation by Dr. Huntoon or another licensed health care professional. Do not begin any health or exercise program without thorough evaluation by a trained health care professional.

Introduction

Why have you chosen this book? Was the title intriguing to you? Have you, like many of us, been searching for answers? Have you been given a difficult set of circumstances that are currently causing you to re-evaluate your life? Are you looking for causes that might explain your difficulties? Is it simply time for you to evolve consciously? Perhaps you are discovering your true life purpose and wish to make a contribution to humanity. Whatever your reason, I am glad you have chosen to read this book.

Let's be clear; your life is 100 % about you, period. That is a bold statement, and perhaps it sounds like a selfish one to you. That doesn't change the fact that your life is 100 % about you. Of course there are others involved in your life. The things we do and do not do will certainly have an effect on others, just as what they do or do not do will have an effect on each of us. And still, your life is 100 % about you. The *Law of Attraction* states that you are the source of your experience. This means that the energy that you transmit results in attracting your experience to you. It doesn't matter what others think or do, your life is still 100 % about you. I can hear you thinking, "...*and what about how others affect my life?*" Sure, you can be affected by others, but that is totally your choice. Being affected by another is a result of freely agreeing with another's perspective. Agreeing with their perspective is an external reflection of some part of you trying to get your attention. Your choices after agreeing with their perspective will be based upon the conclusions you have drawn within yourself. All of this is based upon your own belief system. You will attract to you those people, situations and circumstances that resonate with the energetic force you are emitting in every moment. You are a magnet, attracting to you everything you are aware of and, more importantly, things you are unaware of.

In addition, as you expand your awareness and increase your consciousness, you will begin to see that you are 100 % responsible for everything you have ever experienced or created. All of this becomes clear on your journey of self realization. You are in the image and likeness of GOD. "*Ye too are Gods.*" More accurately stated, you are a part of, or an extension of GOD. You have become individuated from and taken on the illusion of being separate from GOD; as well as separate from anything you perceive to be outside of your physical body. This is an effort for your individuated self (your higher self) to discover who you really are, and that will enable you to evolve back to the source of all that is. The sooner you can get up to speed with this "truth," the sooner your life can begin to play out in a more agreeable fashion.

We all experience limited consciousness throughout our lives. Each of us currently has limited consciousness in many areas, while we believe we fully understand other things. This is always evolving. For example, just a few short years ago the concept of a cell phone didn't even exist. Once the idea was born, it was shared, pursued and developed. It evolved from a 'bag' phone with a huge battery and limited range to the much smaller communication device with huge memories and thousands of applications that we use today. In addition, the cell phone will continue to evolve for some time to come. Now I could have used any of the most recent technological breakthroughs that make our lives easier as an example, but for most of you reading this, the cell phone is easiest to relate to. After all, it is probably our generation who will choose to develop the tools of self empowerment I will be sharing in the coming pages.

Taking the time to increase our consciousness is part of our own evolution as spiritual beings. It is our responsibility. Since everything in our lives is currently speeding up, the rate at which we choose to become conscious must also increase. Fortunately or unfortunately, the rate at which we turn and go with the increased flow, is directly related to the experiences in our lives. When we say "*Yes*" to our lives, things move fast. When we say "*No*", things become problematic.

Time is moving faster and faster each year, and this is directly related to the increase in consciousness we are all experiencing. Eventually we will learn that the ever present moment of now is all there is. Time will cease to exist as we know it. We will finally be able to expand our conscious awareness enough so we can hold all of time at once within our consciousness; instead of experiencing it through our brains one moment at a time in a linear fashion. We currently process information one bit or piece at a time. It is this linear means of processing that creates the illusion of time. As our conscious awareness expands and we are able to process many things at once, the concept of time will ultimately end. We will have become fully conscious beings and will be able to experience anything we choose to, at any moment without limitation. All of this will occur because we will no longer be thinking in a limited way. We will finally be "*all knowing*" and without limitation. For me, this is exciting. It excites me to have no time boundaries and I am eager to share this experience.

Some of the tools I will be describing are designed to help you identify where you are in your conscious evolution now. All of the tools and exercises are intended to increase your level of conscious awareness about yourself. As a result of using these tools and exercises to create conscious change in your life, your life will become easier and more enjoyable. You will be more aligned with your *Source Energy*. That alignment reduces the time it takes to understand what you want; just as time itself is speeding up. The trial and error we all experience in "*learning*" how to deal with life will become less arduous. Each of us will return to our true selves as we express our new authentic self in every moment of now. Once you choose to embark on this journey, you will be able to raise your conscious awareness to the level of Creator – you will become the Conscious Creator and that is our mission, together.

I have spent the better part of 45 years looking for solutions to my life and ways to change my experiences in this world for the better. Many mentors have helped me learn along the way. Also, like any student, I have learned through my own trial and error. I imagine your life has been much of the same. Why else would you be holding this book?

The major discovery I have made is the process by which *evolving consciousness* takes place. Evolving Consciousness is a term I coined to describe how each of us becomes more conscious of our spiritual self, even if we reject the notion that we are spirits in physical form. I use the term Un-consciousness in the sense that we can be unaware of the fact that we are spiritual beings in physical form and even go as far as denying that fact. If this is your current perspective, this is your truth. From an evolving consciousness standpoint in the physical world of our 3rd dimension, this is correct.

Picture a scale of consciousness starting at zero and moving up the scale to infinity. Can we say that beginning at zero consciousness or Un-consciousness is a place for each of us to start? Does it make sense that, if we have had an experience at some point in our 'past', we bring the experience of Un-consciousness full circle by watching someone else have their own experience of being Un-conscious? An example might be watching someone do a task for the first time while we have done it many times. They are 'Un-conscious' as to how to perform the task.

Each time I become aware of the desire for change within my life is ask a question of myself. That question is: *Is there something I do not presently know or understand, the knowing or understanding of which could change everything?* The answer from my perspective is always YES. And when I answer the question with *My Yes*, I open myself up and expand my conscious awareness in my present environment. A sense of calmness always comes over me as I begin to notice things in my environment that I wasn't aware of before. It is as if I open a door to an expanded reality that enables me to see other possibilities and solutions to my current circumstances. I receive new information I wasn't aware of; yet those possibilities and solutions were always there. They were simply hidden from my ability to "see" them because I had not allowed myself to experience that level of awareness. Saying "Yes" opens me up to an expanded conscious awareness. Everyone can do this, and I believe others will benefit from knowing this.

I have used that method of expanding my awareness of my environment for several years and each time I do, I get a sense of calmness in spite of what is going on around me. An additional bonus for me is that, as I have taught this theory to members of my practice and others who have taken my *Quantum Leap© Seminar*, I have seen my world become more calm and easy as a result.

Sharing this information in this format will allow me to touch more people's lives. Your world and mine will become more calm and peaceful. I invite you to have your own experience using this material and I encourage you to connect with me through my *Quantum Leap© Seminar*, by calling me at my office or sending me an e-mail. Let us all continue to evolve, Consciously.

Remember this: *Your choices of action may be limited; BUT your choices of thought are not.*

Dedication & Thanks

For You Who Seek Peace From Within

I am grateful for so many people in my life, those of the past, my present life and of course those who will come into my life in my future. I understand the connection we all serve and I am grateful to all of you who have helped me co-create my experiences through my spiritual process.

Thank You Mom and Dad who agreed to create me so I could have the experience of life itself. Your guidance and nurturing were key to developing my focus. Giving me three brothers allowed me to discover my life purpose. Raising me how you did enabled me to discover my inner strengths, of which have served me well throughout my life. Again, from My Heart, Thank You.

Thank You Mark, David and Keith. Growing up with you as my brothers taught me how to get along with others and showed me and continues to show me what family is all about. The experiences we co-created held and continue to hold many of life's discoveries for me, all of which I continue to carry with me consciously. From My Heart, Thank You.

Thank You to all of my formal teachers for which several had a huge impact in my life and I am eternally grateful for sharing your experience and passion with me. Included are Jim Townsend, Lawrence Carr, Dr. Bernadine Allen, Dr. Phillip Maffetone, Dr. Robert Beck, Dr. Frederick Hult, Dr. Steven Goodstein, Dr. Loren Marks, Sara Rubin, Dr. George Goodheart, Dr. Victor Frank, Dr.'s Scott and Deb Walker, Dr. Leslie Feinberg, and Dr. Doug Gilbert. Each of you have helped me develop my skills as a doctor and as a person by nurturing me to see beyond what is tangential in my world. You taught me to see beyond the physical and into what is possible. You helped me to stretch my boundaries and move into my undiscovered. You, each in your own way, helped to sharpen my skill at discerning my truth. You have my eternal gratitude for being my mentors and friends, as well as my teachers. Thank You.

Thank You to all my new brothers and sisters of the published book fellowship whose previously published works have touched my life and helped to shape my place in the world. You have inspired me to be a better person through your literary style and subjects, and have served as my mentors for the books I am writing. This list includes and is certainly more than this; Neale Donald Walsch for *Conversations with GOD* and everything else you have written, as well as attending several seminars and retreats with you; Esther and Jerry Hicks with *Abraham* and many of your books, audio and video works including *Ask and It Is Given*; Gregg Braden for *The Divine Matrix* and *The Spontaneous Healing of Belief*; Bruce Lipton, PhD for *Biology of Belief*; Robert Tennyson Stevens for *Conscious Language: The Logos of Now* and *Sacred Body Language Translations*; James Redfield for *The Celestine Prophecy* and *The Celestine Prophecy Movie*; Dr. Wayne Dyer for your body of work and seminars.

Finally, I thank all of my practice members for continually looking to me for guidance and inspiration. You are my family who has taught me humility. Your health challenges motivate me to no end and encourage me to find the answers to why you have your concerns. You continue to inspire me to look beyond your condition and see you as whole and healed, which keeps me searching for truth. Now and always am I indebted to you for your countless gifts you have given me through allowing me to help you. Thank You with all my heart.

Quantum Leap©

The information you hold in your hands has been consciously designed to help you, regardless of where you are in your life process, and to allow you to make a **Quantum Leap**© forward on your Spiritual or *Soul* path. We are all here to have an experience, through the lifetimes of our Soul's existence. We have dropped into this arena called "*duality*" and have experienced infinite creative outcomes on the ever-expanding scale of consciousness. All of these experiences are specific to help each of us discover *who we really are*, and, at the same time define *who we choose to be*. As the cycle of duality comes to a close, many of us are finding it harder and harder to overcome our previous cycles of creation; what some call our *Karma*. Many are now beginning to become conscious of this concept, and are starting to wonder, "*Can I make it (clear my Karma) before the cycle is over?*"

Man has for millennia tried to come up with a solution to the ever-increasing difficulties we face, in an effort to overcome suffering through the levels of consciousness. I have had the pleasure of studying with many of these innovators. I have studied the disciplines of Buddhism, read all of Neale Donald Walsch's *Conversations with God* books, and taken several seminars with him. I have listened to and read much of Dr. Wayne Dyer's work, as well as taken seminars with him. I have studied the work of Dr. David R. Hawkins in his *Power vs. Force*, and Hale Dwoskin's *The Sedona Method*. Through Esther and Jerry Hicks, I have read, listened to and practiced the *Teachings of Abraham*. I have even had the opportunity to speak with *Abraham*. I have also practiced Alternative and Energetic Healing techniques in my professional practice for 20 years. My methods of practice include Dr. George Goodheart's *Applied Kinesiology*, Dr. Dick Versandaal's *Contact Reflex Analysis*, Dr. Victor Frank's *Total Body Modification*, Dr. Scott Walker's *Neuro Emotional Technique*, Dr. Leslie Feinberg's *Neuro Modulation*

Technique, Dr. Randy Frank's *Natural Healing*, Dr. Devi Nambudripad's *Nambidripad Allergy Elimination Technique*, and Dr. John Velthiem's *BodyTalk*, and, most recently, the work of Dr. Doug Gilbert. As a result, I am pleased to introduce the culmination of all my years of experience, which has lead me to the process of **Quantum Leap**©.

My hope is that this information will allow you to make a shift in the way you currently think about your life, enabling you to see things in a new way, thus allowing you to do things differently. My goal is to help you make a shift out of your old negative Core Belief patterns and transform you into a consciousness that results in new positive outcomes. My intention is to help you *reprogram* your current Un-conscious way of thinking and reacting to your world in its present form and to help you to make a **Quantum Leap**© in your consciousness to the level you would choose on the Scale of Consciousness. This is a chance to upgrade your present reality with a new, more conscious way of thinking.

When you choose to create your world consciously, instead of reacting, (meaning *to act again* under the influence of a stimulus or prompting) I see all of us living with the empowerment we are all given, but do not know how to express. My intention is to allow positive change for our world and our group consciousness.

Thank You for the opportunity to assist you on your journey. It is an honor and a privilege to help facilitate your process.

Consciously Yours;

Richard A. Huntoon, D.C.

I believe that in order to go someplace new, you must know where you are first. Once you know where you are, then you need a clear picture of where you'd like to be. In an effort to help you focus on that, it is important to have full understanding of what both *conscious* and *Un-conscious* mean. Then we can have a better grasp of what we are going for and will better recognize our results when we finally get there.

The following is the definition of Un-conscious. It is important to fully comprehend the definition of this word so you can understand how it applies throughout this playbook. While creating your life more consciously, you will learn the importance of understanding what each word means when choosing your vocabulary.

un·con·scious
–adjective
1. not conscious; without awareness, sensation, or cognition.

2. temporarily devoid of consciousness.

3. not perceived at the level of awareness; occurring below the level of conscious thought: *an Un-conscious impulse.*

4. not consciously realized, planned, or done; without conscious volition or intent: *an Un-conscious social slight.*

5. not endowed with mental faculties: *the Un-conscious stones.*

–noun
6. the Un-conscious, *Psychoanalysis.* the part of the mind containing psychic material that is ***only rarely accessible to awareness but that has a pronounced influence on behavior.***

Origin:
1705–15; 1915–20 for def. 6; un-¹ + conscious

Conscious is defined below. This word is of equal significance because it is what we all hope to have more of in our lives. After all, being conscious allows us to have more control over how life is happening. More importantly, it allows us to direct our lives to our desired outcomes.

Appreciate the definition of conscious and see all the different ways you can become more conscious as you move through this playbook.

con·scious

–adjective

1. aware of one's own existence, sensations, thoughts, surroundings, etc.

2. fully aware of or sensitive to something (often fol. by *of*): *conscious of one's own faults; He wasn't conscious of the gossip about his past.*

3. having the mental faculties fully active: *He was conscious during the operation.*

4. known to oneself; felt: *conscious guilt.*

5. aware of what one is doing: *a conscious* liar.

6. aware of oneself; self-conscious.

7. deliberate; intentional: *a conscious insult; a conscious effort.*

8. acutely aware of or concerned about: *money-conscious; a diet-conscious society.*

9. *Obsolete.* inwardly sensible of wrongdoing.

–noun

10. the conscious, *Psychoanalysis.* the part of the mind comprising psychic material **_of which the individual is aware._**

Origin:

1625–35; < L *conscius* sharing knowledge with, equiv. to *con-* con- + *sci-* (s. of sc□re to know; see science) + *-us* -ous; cf. nice

Now that we are clear about these two definitions, please take the time to think about each when exploring the tools and moving through the exercises. By being conscious of all your senses when working with this material will allow your transformative process to occur in a more agreeable fashion. When one is in agreement, things move faster. Best of outcomes to you.

Statement of Outcome

My outcome for sharing *Quantum Leap*© with you is:

- You upgrade at least one major glitch in your current Core Belief System as early as TODAY. This will depend on how fast you apply the information.

- You have powerful tools to take with you, and integrate into your current life creating the conscious change you wish to experience.

- You interact with your world with more clarity and vision than you have ever imagined before today.

- You have a path available on which you acquire even more powerful tools for upgrading your life.

- You listen consciously to your own *Internal Guidance* (your connection to GOD, the Divine, the Universe, or whatever name you desire).

- You remember *Who You Really Are.*

- You remember how powerful and creative you are, because you are *Creator.*

Contents

Margin Noting

Margin noting is a simple, efficient and effective technique, which can be used to remain fully and completely present in a classroom setting or while studying and learning written material.

At times, the conscious mind can be distracted by a bodily sensation, a memory, an image, or a noise. Persistent thoughts or distractions are what margin noting addresses. If a thought or feeling continues to pull at one's attention, it is usually because the subconscious mind requires some kind of attention, usually in reference to what the distraction is about. This is especially true during experiences like *Quantum Leap©* or other Life Improvement courses or seminars, where highly charged memories and feelings are brought to the surface for transformation.

Margin noting is done by jotting down a quick note of key words or a short sentence to remind you about what the distraction was. By writing down a margin note, one's subconscious mind is acknowledged and satisfied that the issue will be dealt with later. This allows the subconscious to relax and wait its turn so to speak. Similar to waiting in line at a crowded deli, once I receive eye contact and some sort of acknowledgement from the server, I relax a bit and am patient knowing I will be served soon, and in order.

It is very important to go back to all your margin notes and facilitate the issue that created the distraction so your subconscious mind will trust you to deal with your stuff. Your margin note is an agreement between your conscious and subconscious minds. If your subconscious trusts you, then it will let go of the distraction, knowing it will have time later.

The topics, words, images, and sounds are sometimes very significant doorways to our own healing, so it is important to give them some consideration later.

When making a margin note, simply write a word or short phrase that captures the essence of the distraction which will serve as a reminder later on when you return to it. Again, it is important to take the time later to deal with the issue that was distracting you and handle it to completion. By keeping your agreement with your subconscious, it will be more inclined to bring matters to your attention knowing they will be dealt with.

Agreements for Being and Using the Material of Quantum Leap©

The following agreements are a commitment to yourself. Agreeing to play by these agreements will align your conscious and subconscious minds to get the greatest results.

1. Play 125 % in every moment of your life (showing up is 100 %. Play full on and go further than you ever thought you could—and then go even further - that is 125 %.)
2. Live your word.
3. Keep your purpose for using this material in focus.
4. Acknowledge that what every person in your life is saying is true for them in that moment.
5. Commit to listening purposefully and being mentally present and focused in your life when other people speak.
6. Be committed to having your highest choice.
7. Be effective and efficient in your thoughts, words and actions.
8. Be willing to win.
9. Allow others to win in their own way.
10. Choose to choose. Come from your heart.
11. Keep all personal information shared in your life confidential.
12. Commit to listen to your Internal Guidance.
13. See only perfection.
14. Relax, receive and give yourself permission to HAVE FUN!

Relax as you learn the information in *Quantum Leap*© to *Transform* Your Life. If you get caught up in the doing it ***"right"*** or ***"wrong"*** then you've missed the point. The point of using this material is to identify and attract your heart's greatest desire for your health and your life by aligning your thoughts, feelings and emotions with your desire. So be gentle with yourself as you learn to focus your words to attract what you choose.

Signed:_____Date:_____

This is a commitment to yourself. By signing and dating this page, you are witnessing your commitment to consciously improve your creative life process.

Road Map For Using This Material

1) <u>Negative State</u>: *Becoming Consciously Aware of the need for Change*

Written Language Entry	Exercise # 1 & # 3	pages 13 & 66
Verbal Language Entry	Limiting Language	pages 44 – 56
Observe the Moment	Toolbox Item # 2	page 59
Releasing	Toolbox Item # 3	page 61
Body Language Entry	Toolbox Item # 5	page 70
Finding Your Negative Core Beliefs	Exercise # 4	page 102

2) <u>Neutral State</u>: *Great start, and no place to BE if you desire TRUE change*

Find the Emotion and Clear it	Energy of Emotions Chart	
What's it turn into?	Toolbox Item # 1	page 30

3) <u>Positive State</u>: *Truly makes your Heart Sing; This is HOME*

Find Focusing Language		page 57
Make New Creative Choice	Energy of Emotions Chart	
What's it turn into?	Toolbox Item # 1	page 30
Decrees to Create New Reality /Feeling State	Toolbox Item # 4	page 63

<u>Support New State: Use Your Tools and Exercises to keep Ongoing Conscious Development</u>

Decrees to Create New Reality/ Feeling State	Toolbox Item # 4	page 63
Decreeing	Exercise # 2	page 66
Your Internal Guidance System	Toolbox Item # 6	page 104
The Freedom Process	Toolbox Item # 7	page 106

The Biology of Belief: Positive Thoughts have a profound effect on behavior and genes but only when they are in harmony with subconscious programming. And negative thoughts have an equally powerful effect. When we recognize how these positive and negative beliefs control our biology, we can use this knowledge to create lives filled with health and happiness.

Bruce Lipton, Ph.D.

Why Are Your Really Here?

Take a few moments to do the following exercise. Think of something you would like to accomplish by reading this book, doing the exercises and then applying the tools to yourself and your life. What would you like to become true as the result of going through this process? Answer this question: Why are you really here reading this book and trying to improve your life? What is the real reason for taking the time and dedicating 125 % effort to improving your life? Your Soul has a purpose for incarnating at this time. What is your purpose/your Soul's purpose for being here? In other words, all life has a purpose and many of us are not conscious of our life's purpose. Take the time to discover that for yourself right now, before going forward with this book. I promise you this: If you take the time to do this exercise, the outcome you achieve as a result of going through this book will be the most profound gift you have ever received. And the best part about it is - you will have given it to yourself.

Take the time to go within yourself and feel, from your heart, what your purpose is. This is not something that will come from your *Thinking Mind*. Thinking is done with your brain and is influenced by your core beliefs, your memory, your ego and your personal laws. It is based upon what you believe you are capable of, or for many it is influenced by what they think they are not capable of. Nor am I asking you to answer the question from your *Emotional Body*. This is the part of you that is on all the time and is done without thinking. I am asking you to get out of your head and move 18 inches below it to your heart. This is your true self, your Eternal Self. What does your heart truly desire to experience and what is your true purpose for being here? This requires you to activate your Higher Self or your Eternal Self. For many, this may be completely foreign. Realize that I just revealed the three voices we hear in our mind as we deal with our lives. Most are aware of and live from the first two and there are actually three. They are as follows:

3 Different Ways of Listening to Yourself:

1. *Emotional Body* – this is automatic, and done without thinking. The quickest way to understand this aspect of listening to yourself is paying attention to your automatic reactions, first thoughts or first words. This is purely instinct and emotion without conscious control of your reactions.

2. *Thinking Mind* – using thought (typical way). This is slower and more deliberate as each of us takes the time to compare what is happening in the NOW to what we have previous experience dealing with in our past. Then we compare the two before we *re-act*. We are given the opportunity to think about our response OR we can simply re-act, as in knowing it is wrong and doing it anyway.

3. *Eternal Self* – here you will find your connection to your *Internal Guidance System*. It requires you to get really present and feel your answers rise to the surface of your consciousness. This type of response is typically very slow in coming and has a different quality then the first two types of reactions. As you "*play*" with this way of responding more and more, you will begin speaking from your heart. People will feel the sincerity of your words and will respond in alignment with your intention.

For now I would like you to take the time to get in touch with your Eternal Self and find out *Why are you really here?* Your answer will feel right and will typically be very simple and brief. It will not require a lot of explanation. It will simply *feel right*. If your answer is a sentence or two long with reasons and justifications for why you feel that way, you are not tapping into your Eternal Self. You are using your Thinking Mind. When accessing your Eternal Self, you will feel the answer come from your heart and slowly move to your conscious awareness. Your answer will usually be limited to one or perhaps two words. And as soon as you speak it out loud, you will feel centered and clear. Play with this and be patient with yourself. The first time I did this was in a group setting and everyone else in the room was intuitively picking up on my answer long before I found it myself. And after 45 minutes, the tiniest of voices was heard from deep within myself and said *"Open My Heart."* And when I finally accepted what I was hearing and spoke it into the room, the energy shifted, everyone said "Yes" and I felt centered for the first time within my body. I truly felt I had found my Soul's Purpose and finally unlocked my heart. Since then, I have found my ability to be centered and connect with others is much easier and much more sincere. I cannot impress upon you enough the importance of taking the time to do this for yourself before going forward with the rest of the coming pages. Resist the urge to go on until you have found your Soul's purpose for being here and for finding this book. You will be eternally changed when you come to discover your true Eternal Self. And you'll be happy you did.

Where Am I?

Before we can determine where we are going, we must understand where we are starting from. I call this "*My Current Reality.*" A simple example is using a GPS System in your car or other mode of transportation, or perhaps using one of the MAP features on the Internet. You have to type in your current position, or where you'd like to start your journey. Once you do that, then you can enter your desired destination and the computer will calculate the route depending on distance, time, traffic and other variables. If you follow the directions given, you will reach your desired destination. Many use these devices or services to be certain they will arrive at their destination. It takes the worry out of the equation. You simply follow the directions, listen to the voice and do what you are told, and *wha-lah*, you arrive at your destination.

The great part of just about all technology used in society today is all of it is based on our nervous system and the various ways it communicates and categorizes. We also have our own GPS System. Our "Emotional Guidance System" or our EGS, helps us determine how we feel about what is going on; as processed through our nervous system and based upon our current belief system. Our EGS controls how we feel about things, what we consider to be possible, what we like, do not like and where we choose to go next; and it is all based on the information stored within our memory. It helps us make our choices in life.

In an effort to access some of what we believe, it is important to determine where we are in relation to our beliefs. In the following exercise, I will ask you to do just that. There are several different topics for you to choose from. Pick the one that elicits the most amount of "charge" for you; the one that causes you to re-act the most. Go through the exercise with this as your topic. Sometimes it might be the one you hope it isn't. Take the time to go through the following exercise to help determine where you are and what your *"Current Reality"* is.

Exercise # 1
My Current Reality

Our words, thoughts and feelings reflect our *"Current Reality."* The words we speak and the thoughts we have can and do influence our feelings and state of being. For instance, *"I am only half the way there"* feels very different than *"I am already half the way there."* *"I don't know"* feels very different than *"I choose to know."* One statement limits action, while the other allows for movement—freeing us up for creating & attracting.

This feeling of movement (of possibility) is important because what we feel affects what we attract. The **Law of Attraction** says that our feelings actually set the frequency for what we attract. If we are feeling anger, then we attract angry people or situations. If we are feeling grateful, then we attract more things to be grateful for. Feeling joy and gratitude are the most powerful states to create more love and abundance in our lives (**The Secret**).

The following exercise helps you find any area in your life where you have been creating and/or attracting situations, feelings or people which **limit your potential** to have what you truly desire in life. I call this state *"Current Reality."* To find out how to get to where you are going, **you first need to know where you are**. I will guide you in finding some of your "current reality" and your current beliefs, which do not serve you.

Circle the topic which elicits the most feeling for you in your *"Current Reality."* When you have completed this, please move forward with this exercise, page 16. Be honest with yourself and choose the one that speaks loudest to you.

Topics

Life is:	My job is:	Sex is:	GOD is:	Food Is:	My body is:
Success is:	Health is:	Love is:	Pleasure is:	Money is:	School is:
Wealth is:	Parenting is:	Emotions are:	Religion is:	Families are:	Diets are:
Fun is:	Parents are:	Spirituality is:	I am:	Poverty is:	My dreams are:
Rich people are:		My relationship with _____ is:			

Remember:

- Use your common, familiar thoughts
- Be spontaneous, it's OK for you to feel your emotions
- Write down your "first words" exactly the way they come into your mind
- Using one-word phrases can be as effective as using complete sentences and thoughts. Mix it up. Believe that whatever you write has a purpose.
- Write from your "Current Reality" or present experience

The following is an example for you to look at to give you more understanding of how to do this exercise. I used the example of "Health is:" since most reading this book will have some level of health challenge. It would have been just as easy to have used any of the other topics. I actually invite you to do this exercise with every topic, as I am certain that each of us has some level of "prejudice" around each. Even if you do not, it will still help you to know your truth by taking the time to look at each.

Example: Health is….

I would ask you to take ownership of "your issue" and make it "**My** Health Is…"

Poor	Good
Bad	Strong
Lacking	Getting Better
In need of attention	Great
Terrible	Important
Failing	Returning
Sorry	Easy
Unsatisfactory	Fun
Confusing	Happy
Complicated	A Joy
Uncomfortable	Up to me
My life	Awesome

Doctor visits

Taking medication

Taking more medication

Requiring surgery

Never good

Always a problem

Difficult

Hard to get right

Out of balance

Getting worse

Sad

In a state of disrepair

Always Getting Stronger

Expanding

Growing

In balance

Appreciate that if you have negative attention on something, and you have an issue with it, then you are thinking negatively about that issue. The more negatives vs. positives you can list, it is likely that your chronic experience of the issue is negative. Taking the time to define how you feel about this issue will allow you to see for yourself why it is a negative experience for you. This is a powerful exercise. Look at every aspect of your life to understand why those aspects are an issue for you. Some will be more than others and all will need attention from time to time. Your objective here is to locate the one which requires the most amount of attention, as it is the one currently pulling on you the most.

<u>**My Current Reality Worksheet**</u>

Topic:_____

Write sentences and words that come to mind for your Topic using both positive and negative feelings: (use the example on the previous page for help getting started)

_____

_____

_____

_____

_____

_____

_____

_____

_____

_____

Pick the one you like the least from above and write a paragraph about how you feel

_____

_____

_____

_____

_____

_____

_____

Save this section for later (Part of Exercise # 3 pg. 66)

**Write your New Upgrade Conscious Choice(s) for your life.
UPGRADING Exercise # 1**

_____

_____

_____

_____

_____

_____

_____

_____

Now that you know where you are, it is important to know how you got there. Throughout this book we will be discussing *Your Core Belief System* and what that does to influence your life. Your *Core Belief System* is the sum total of all your beliefs and how those beliefs, stored in your Un-conscious mind, determine how you experience your life. We will also learn that it is through your beliefs that you attract or reject all of your experiences. You create your experiences because of your beliefs. The experiences you have in your life are based upon the most powerful law in the universe. This law is *The Law of Attraction.* This is important to understand. We will take the time to learn about this all-important law; how it is always at work and how you are always using it, whether you are conscious of it or not. Once you understand how it works, you can begin to search out the Core Beliefs you now have that are limiting your enjoyment of life. Then you can transform those limited beliefs into unlimited potential. Once you begin to see the unlimited potential that is your birthright, you will begin to shift your belief system from one that is limited and lacking to one of expansiveness and expression - manifesting all your hearts true desires.

We activate *The Law of Attraction* through our intention, which we all use all the time, both consciously and Un-consciously. It is *The Law of Attraction.* This universal, all powerful law always brings that which is your dominant vibration. This consists of everything that is held in our mind, both in our conscious awareness and in our Un-conscious awareness. We will learn that 95% to 99 % of our day is spent Un-consciously. It is important to learn how to expand our consciousness so we can move consciously into our Un-conscious awareness and allow ourselves to become fully conscious beings. As a fully conscious being, we will become the conscious creator of our experience and thus be able to create anything we choose. Since this has always been our God given right, why not take advantage of it? Let us learn about this all powerful, always functioning law of the universe; *The Law of Attraction.*

The Law of Attraction

Most of this book is about focusing your intent and feelings through your words in order to use *The Law of Attraction* in your own life. *The Law of Attraction* is comprised of three steps:

1. Ask with Feeling
2. Your Universe Answers
3. Receive

I will show you how to use your words to align your Un-conscious mind with your conscious desires to accomplish all three steps successfully. I invite you to learn this information for yourself and to then share it with your loved ones and others you interact with on a regular basis. This will increase the success of your results and help improve your life.

Our Conscious Mind

The *Conscious* Mind refers to our mind when we are focused on who we are right now and what we are doing right now. This is the mind referred to in *The Power of Now* (E. Tolle). The more we stay in our "*now,*" the more focused we are in choosing what we attract into our lives and create from moment to moment.

Even when we are completely focused on our "*now,*" our Un-conscious minds are still running, keeping our bodily functions going for us. We do not need to pay attention to keeping our heart beating or digesting our food. When balanced and integrated, our conscious and Un-conscious minds work together in powerful accord, creating what we choose in our lives.

Focus

What we focus on consciously AND
Un-consciously is what we attract to ourselves.

To focus means literally "*an act of concentrating interest or activity on something.*" To be focused is to concentrate on what you are doing, seeing, hearing, smelling, tasting, touching and/or feeling. Being focused involves using all of your senses; it involves a level of presence where you are aware of yourself and your surroundings with full clarity.

According to *The Law of Attraction*, what we focus on consciously AND Un-consciously is what we attract to us. In our lives, if we focus on our hurdles (lack, limitation, struggle, disease) or what we do NOT desire, we will tend to create or attract situations with more of the same hurdles. As I am sure you have experienced that more than once, I invite you to focus to the best of your ability on the positive. As you spend more time practicing this while going through the book, you will begin to naturally do this as easily as you currently notice the negative more.

Let us begin with the following question:

What Is Your Focus?

We are always focused on the Past, the Present or the Future. That focus is either Positive or Negative. Acknowledging that all of your power is here in the Present, (unless, of course, it is not focused in the Present) you can choose to focus on the Present either Positively or Negatively. What you focus on, Positively or Negatively, is what you will experience. If you think bad things will happen, bad things will usually happen. If you think good things will happen, good things will most likely happen. Your ability to focus on 'good' or 'bad' will determine your outcomes. Your ability to have all of your focus in the present and to be present with all your thoughts will allow you to set your intention on whatever you want to create. Since the Universe functions on *The Law of Attraction* which says, "*Like attracts like,*" what you attract into your life will be based upon the energy you radiate. What you put out based upon your focus, Positive or Negative, is what you will draw to yourself and what will become your reality. What if you focus 20 % of your attention in the positive and 80 % in the negative? What will happen then? If it is the other way around, 80 % positive and 20 % negative. What do you think the result will be? It is likely that your outcome will be in alignment with your focus.

Remember that what your life has been up to this point in time influences how you see your world today. You navigate your life based upon your past experiences. They have shaped your perspective and impacted your choices and decisions. As a result, you are making choices based upon your past conditioning either Un-consciously or consciously. Your conscious choices will usually turn out better than those that are based on your Un-conscious. Most of your Un-conscious choices are based on suppressed negative emotion. It is because of those that you focus on the past. If you try to create from that space, you will create based upon the energy of your current thoughts, as well as thoughts from the past. These thoughts are usually founded in suppressed negative emotion. Who would want those outcomes?

Your focus is what it is all about. What you focus on is what you will begin to resonate. *The Law of Attraction* will then pull toward you those circumstances, situations, people and things on which you are focusing. If you divide your focus i.e. have two different thoughts/emotions that are oppositional like joy and fear, you will allow your primary focus to prevail. Very basically, this is what it is all about. You can bring about anything you would like, simply (not really) by focusing, single mindedly, on that which you choose to have happen or be.

How do you keep from splitting your focus?

Focusing, single mindedly on anything is not easy, but focus can be learned if you practice. Stay present with what is happening now and hold one positive thought in your mind for a minimum of 17 seconds. Then begin to build on that one thought by adding other positive thoughts. Choose these other thoughts in alignment with your original dominant positive thought and hold the total for an additional 17 seconds. If you can continually focus this way for more than 68 seconds (or four 17 second cycles adding 4 positive thoughts to your original thought) things in your reality will begin to physically shift. Things will change. The things you begin to experience will be those positive things on which you have single-mindedly focused. This focus, in our current state of consciousness, is not an easy task. With practice, however, this will be more productive than any physical activity you under take.

How does this impact Your Health?

Understand that any and all health issues are absolutely a byproduct of negative focus. This can be Short-term intense acute focus, or a more subtle long-term chronic focus.

Let's assume you have a health issue in your life, whether acute or chronic, that you don't care for. The best question to ask yourself is, "What is bothering me?" Your natural response may be obvious, meaning something like "This pain is what is bothering me." What I'd like you to accept is that the pain you are feeling is a symptom of something else. Consider the pain as a physical representation of what is bothering you. So again, ask, *"What is it that is bothering me that I am not able to resolve in my life and in my head?" "What am I resisting, fighting, pushing against or being controlled by that is bothering me?" "What am I not happy with?" "What life circumstance is causing me to think negatively?"* This can be anything causing frustration, anger, fear, sadness or other similarly negative emotions. These are important questions to ask yourself with any health related issue, regardless of how acute or chronic your condition may be. If you are always focused in a negative way, as a result of an issue remaining in your life that currently has power over you, it will continually create negative focus consciously and/or Un-consciously. If you can't seem to overcome or resolve it in your favor you will cause your body to develop a health imbalance. You might be thinking now**, "***Oh, it's my job, my duties at work, my husband, my wife, my neighbor, my boss, my co-worker, my child.***"** Be honest. What circumstance in your life is bothering you causing your physical complaint? You must identify your issue first. You probably did that in the first exercise called "*Your Current Reality.*" Once you can identify what that is, then we will learn how to let that go.

When you resist something, you keep it planted in your life. If you have a negative thought or emotion about someone, or something, you hold onto that circumstance. As your negative thoughts/feelings continue or when you have to deal with someone or something on a regular basis, you continue to focus on the negative emotion that you don't want to think about. This can occur consciously, but more commonly, it occurs Un-consciously. As a result, the negative energy (emotion) associated with your circumstance causes your body to build physical resistance to your situation; and this creates physical reactions resulting in pain or other health issues. Acute circumstances of highly intense negative energy/emotion will cause acute symptoms. More common outcomes are chronic health issues; cancers, heart disease and other degenerative conditions that result from low-grade chronic negative energy/emotion. Throughout our lives everyone experiences this cycle. If we're lucky, however, we learn to *Quantum Leap©* out of our negative thought patterns. That is the reason for this book, and this material. I want to teach you how to make that *Quantum Leap©* into Health and Happiness that may not exist in your life today.

What Might You Consider Doing?

First you have to determine what you'd like to experience. You might say, "*Well that's easy. I want to not have pain!*" "*I want to feel good, feel better.*" That in itself is easy to accomplish conceptually, but it will require some specific focus in order to experience it within you physically. It will require some disciplined thinking about something other than the pain or discomfort. It will require you to think about your health returning and focus on how that feels. This leads us to the introduction of some powerful laws that we all operate from.

THE ART OF MANIFESTING

Your ability to understand and apply these four components will allow you to reveal anything you desire. Most notably, this will allow you to change your health to the type of health you'd like in the shortest amount of time possible. If you have questions, make your margin notes and then contact me as I am happy to assist you to better understanding.

THE LAW OF ATTRACTION

As we've discussed earlier, this law states: *that which is likened to itself is drawn.* You draw everything you think and feel to yourself. You are a magnet attracting positive and/or negative events through your thoughts, words and deeds. Each is based on your feelings and emotions which support your thoughts. The more constant you hold your feelings and emotions, the more you will turn them into your reality. Positive or negative, the results will speak for what your thoughts and feelings are and have been. Don't like the outcomes/results of your present life? Then change your thoughts and feelings. Change your thoughts and feelings, and you will change your life.

THE LAW OF DELIBERATE CREATION

This is about wanting to create on purpose; it actually is *The Law of Creation*. It feeds off *The Law of Attraction*. It works based on your thoughts, whether you embrace what you are thinking or not. If you are thinking of things you *don't* want, you are giving that thought power, and *The Law of Attraction* will then bring it to you. Likewise, if you hold the thought you do wish to experience, you will draw it to you through your intention. Always take action in joy. Think, see and expect positives to BE, and they will BE. *The Law of Attraction* says so.

THE LAW OF ALLOWING

I am that which I am, and I am pleased with it, joyful with it. In addition, I am able to allow that which you are and allow myself to be pleased with it, joyful with it. I understand that if I am able to allow by offering no resistance to what is, then it will sponsor positive feelings and thus allow *The Law of Attraction* and *Deliberate*

Creation to bring my desires to me. This doesn't work if you are simply tolerating the circumstances. You will need to allow them without resistance.

SEGMENT INTENDING

When you stop to identify what you are choosing to display, you can focus emphasis and power to create that which you are ***intending***. You are preparing your future in segments that are consciously intended. Your focused intention will allow you to create that which you are intending by choice. The time delay between your intention and the physical manifestation is based upon the amount of resistance you offer to your intended creation. This is based on the emotional reality of your subject, and influenced by your conscious and/or Un-conscious emotional reality.

YOUR EMOTIONAL GUIDANCE SYSTEM

This is your *Inner Guidance* that comes from your Inner Being, the core of who you really are. It is based upon all your positive and negative emotions, conscious and/or Un-conscious. If you can be open to becoming aware of how you are feeling in this moment in time and allow yourself to become conscious of what you are feeling, you can begin to consciously change your thoughts to more positive ones. This will allow you to create more positive outcomes through your new conscious positive focus. If you are thinking and feeling negative emotions, consciously or Un-consciously, you will tend to create more negative outcomes.

THE TIME DELAY

The time between your thoughts and the manifestation of your thoughts in physical reality is a bi-product of your ability to offer *pure positive emotion* **a**nd hold onto your positive thoughts for a minimum of 17 seconds. For every successive 17 seconds you can focus positively, will sponsor another positive thought to go with it. This will be the equivalent of many thousands of hours of physical creating. Holding a focused positive thought for 68 seconds, or four 17 second intervals, will allow you to see physical changes in your environment. This is how manifestation works.

Our Un-Conscious Minds

Our Un-conscious mind keeps every component of ourselves running 24/7 whether we are paying attention or not. It keeps our hearts beating and our body temperature normal. It checks for danger constantly, based on our driving instinct to survive. It monitors everything happening around us through all of our senses and compares them with what has happened in our past. This is the basis for *Re-Acting*, as we compare what is happening to what has happened. Our Un-conscious mind is "*programmed*" to distinguish safety from danger by the time we are 6 years old, and this enables us to live to reproductive age. (Bruce Lipton, Ph. D. *The Biology of Belief*).

What Happens When Our Un-conscious Mind Runs Our Show?

Depending on our situation, many of us live our lives acting like two different people. One is our personality when we are relaxed and fully present, focused on what we are doing and who we really are (this is our *conscious self*). Studies show that most people are conscious somewhere between 1 – 5 % of the time. This means that our Un-conscious mind (aka *auto pilot*) runs the show 95 – 99 % of the time.

Note: This explains why, in the early stage of a relationship we can act one way and later behave like someone else entirely. When we first enter a relationship, we are focused and present, being our conscious selves. After some time, when we get distracted by our daily routines, we begin to participate only partially in the relationship in the present. It seems to our partners as if we are taking them for granted. Our Un-conscious minds take over.

Programming our "Beliefs"

The Un-conscious mind is almost completely "*programmed*" by age 6, and contains most of the information needed for the person to survive in their environment. Everything that happens, everything we experience, everything we are told about life, about money, about relationships, work, and GOD, gets "*programmed*" directly into our Un-conscious mind and becomes our "*set of beliefs*", or our "*belief system.*" These beliefs which are created during this time are used by us as "*filters*" as we encounter life. Information coming to us from our outside world goes through our *filters* and is compared to what we "*believe to be possible.*" Anything which falls outside of "*possible*" based on our *Belief System* is rejected by us and we won't see, hear or experience whatever it is (*The Biology of Belief*). Both conscious and Un-conscious minds are affected by our *old programming*.

Our Programming/Core Belief System - Our Basis For Limitation

We are taught "*You too can do all this and more*" and yet we don't seem to experience this in our everyday lives. There is a very good reason for this. Please consider the following information and then ask yourself if what is being said is true for you.

We are the sum total of all our worldly experiences. There is a lot that goes into that statement. We are the sum total of all our *preconceived notions* (pre-conditioning) about who we are. These are based on 1) what we've been taught by our parents (family lineage) and other authorities in our lives: government, police, teachers, the media, mentors, friends and peer-groups (known as *our programming*) and 2) our own trial and error, or our personal experiences. Our choice of experiences is a result of our internal desires and yearnings for knowledge of life. This is in conjunction with, and in spite of, our pre-conditioning. As a result, we develop our own *Personal Laws.*

Our *Personal Laws* are what we believe to be possible or not possible *for us.* These are our unique *Beliefs* which become, over time, our *Core Belief System.* This governs our behavior in the face of life. Our *Personal Laws* exist and are the result of both our Positive and Negative *Core Belief System.* Our beliefs were programmed into most of us before we knew better (age 6) or had enough of our own personal life experience to decide differently. Also, there is an underlying desire, our *Soul's desire,* to experience more of life than we believe is possible by our current reality. This is a driving force and the reason life continues to evolve and upgrade. This is why life moves along in spite of our Negative Core Belief System.

Repetition Compulsion

Have you ever wondered why each of us continues to fall into the same old trap of life repeating itself? Have you ever known that you are continuing a particular habit of life repeating itself over and over again, in spite of all your attempts to change things? Sometimes the people involved change, or we change the components, but the patterns themselves always seem to be there. One of my mentors has called this repeating process, the *Repetition Compulsion* cycle of *self-sabotage.* There are several different ways we seek help if we have become aware enough to know we have a repetitious pattern in life and desire to change. Frequently you'll find yourself in a Psychiatrist's office, or another office designed to help you understand yourself on a deeper level and support your desire for change. You can spend countless hours and financial resources discussing your behavior, and the "*possible*" reasons you behave in that manner. Moreover, you can even feel good about getting to the place where you recognize your behavior and the underlying reasons for it. I am reminded of Richard Gere in the movie *Pretty Woman* where he says to Julia Robert's character, "It took me several years of therapy to be able to say, 'I am very angry with my father.'" And so you can do that form of therapy and get good results to be able to recognize your issue. Then what do you do? *How do you truly re-solve the behavior and eliminate the habit pattern, creating a new, more desired outcome? How do you reprogram your Negative Core Belief System?*

Since all of these patterns are ingrained in your sub-conscious/Un-conscious mind, they are hard to change. By definition, your sub-conscious/Un-conscious mind is *not part of your consciousness.* It is the part of your mind that is below your level of conscious perception. In other words, you are not consciously aware of it. This is the reason for the limitations in our life; our *Un-conscious Core Belief System.*

If most of our choices or our *re-actions* to life are coming from our preconditioned subconscious/Un-conscious mind, how can the cycle be broken? Begin by looking at your words. Our words are a window into our Un-conscious mind. The phrases we choose are clues to what is going on in our Un-conscious mind. There are also mannerisms and body language. Before we get into those, let us begin with our words.

Our Words

Words are powerful. They can create or destroy. Choose your words wisely and be conscious of what you are building or tearing down with them.

The words we say, the phrases we use and the way we speak them represent who we are. Remember, however, that who we are can always be upgraded to who we choose to be. We can use our language in two different ways:

1. Automatic Language: *Un-conscious Limiting Language*

   This is comprised of words we use when we are not focused on our conversation. They are often reflections of our Un-conscious beliefs. We use those words to find the Un-conscious agreements we have made in our lives which stifle creativity. This is called "*Limiting Language*" and it attracts what we are Un-consciously agreeing to because of our beliefs.

2. Focusing Language: *Use of Your Words to Focus Your Intent*

   Speak consciously, with feeling and use words that define what you choose to come into your existence. Remember the *Law of Attraction* and attract only what you desire with the words you use. Our thoughts and words can change our focus from what we do not desire to what we choose to attract. This is done with conscious focus and intent.

Note: An example; if you say "_not too bad_" in an automatic response to someone asking "_How are you?_" you might consciously say to yourself, "_Oops, I focus ONLY on what I choose to attract._" Then you can consciously upgrade your response and say "_Cancel that, I am doing GREAT._" Remember, your thoughts and your words focus and create your feelings, which are crucial to attracting what you desire (_The Law of Attraction_).

Toolbox Item # 1
Energy of Emotions

This is the beginning of upgrading your language to focus your intent. Using focusing language to create what you truly desire is a powerful way to help move from Neutral to First Gear...Fast!

- Emotions each have a specific energetic frequency.
- Energy cannot be eliminated or destroyed—but it can be _transformed_
- Use _Focusing Language_ to transform _Limiting Language/Emotions_ into what you desire.
- Here _Limiting Energy_ is represented by _Limiting Language_, which often goes along with a specific _Limiting Emotion_. For example, the phrase "_I can't_" or "_it's too hard._" is often indicative of apathy.

3 Step Process

1. Find a negative emotion and if you can recall, the original time you felt this way.
2. Find out what Creative Choice it turns into.
3. Decree Your New State.

Energy of Emotions

Emotions have Energy. For anyone who has ever felt fear, this is easy to understand. Originally, emotions were meant to motivate for survival purposes. Now emotions still motivate us, and when we learn how to use them to create what we choose in our lives, we increase our ability to attract what we desire. If we identify the emotion, recognize the energy behind the emotion (the reason), and transform it into an emotional energy that matches it AND Focuses Our Intent, then we can transform a limiting energy into a creative choice. Creative Choice focuses our intent and is key to attracting our desires.

Chart of Improved Outcomes: Based On Creative Choice
ENTHUSIASM

Enthusiasm, Ecstasy, Gratitude, Inspired, Passionate, Creative, Joy

Enthusiasm is the Energy of Creation, Attraction and Manifestation. It generates a higher energy than any other emotion.
Decree Examples: "I enjoy my life." "I feel my joy in my new house." "I joyfully create…"

Category of Emotions →	Limiting Energy →	Improved Outcomes/Creative Choice	
PAIN		**Love &/or Intuition Returning**	H
Physical or Emotional Pain	**It Hurts**	"I surrender to my feelings."	I
Hate		"I accept my intuition & love."	G
ANGER		**Authority, Loving Action**	H
Resentment, Frustration, Rage	**They did this to me; It's their fault I…**	**Authorship Returning**	E
Aggression, Irritation, Bitter,	Anger upgrades **THROUGH**	"I forgive my Mom for… and I	R
Aggravating, Defensive,	**FORGIVENESS** into **AUTHORITY**	have my authority to…"	
Betrayed, Stubborn, Pessimism		"I am in control of my…"	E
FEAR		**Trust, Confidence, Courage,**	N
Dread, Paralyzed Will, Scared	**I'm scared, I'm worried, I'm afraid**	**Faith & Security Returning**	E
Impending Doom, Worried,		"I have my courage to…"	R
Wishy-Washy, Distrust, Blame		"I trust I am secure."	G
Vulnerable, Insecure, Lost		"I'm confident that I can…"	Y
GRIEF		**Joy, Happiness, Cheerfulness**	L
Sadness, Yearning, Anguish	**I always; Things never work out**	**Amused, Delight Returning**	O
Embarrassment, Dogmatic, Guilt	Absolutes/Grandiose words	"I accept what is, and I feel my joy	W
Crying, Depression, Shameful	Usually denotes Grief	at learning…from my situation."	
Humiliation, Wounded Pride		**Pride, Honor Returning**	E
Mortification, Awkwardness		"I am proud of my choices."	R
APATHY		**Ease, Caring, Clarity Returning**	E
Low Self-Esteem, Disgust		"I choose to make it easy."	N
Lack of Control, Depressed	**I can't; It's too hard**	"GOD in me can."	E
Hopeless, Confused, Overwhelmed		"I choose my clarity."	R
UNCONSCIOUS		**Consciousness & Feeling Returning**	G
Numb, Lack of Feeling	**I don't know; I don't understand**	"I choose I am conscious of…NOW!"	Y

Focus Your Intent by Using Decrees: To decree means *"to state with feeling."* As you decree yourself into your new state, make sure the energy of your Creative Choice matches the emotion you started with.
Remember, this is about "convincing" your unconscious mind you ARE in your new state of being.
If you decree authority with the energy level of courage, you will not convince yourself.
Above Fear tend to create Co-Empowered Relationships
Below Fear tend to create Co-Dependent Relationships
Borrowed from Dr. Doug Gilbert in his "Re-Write Your Rules" Seminar

The Emotional Scale

100

Joy: a condition or feeling of great pleasure or happiness; delight. A source of pleasure

Knowledge: the state or fact of knowing; familiarity, awareness, or understanding through experience. The sum or range of what has been perceived, discovered or learned.

Empowerment: to promote the self-actualization or influence of

Freedom: the power to act, speak or think without externally imposed restraints; immunity from obligation.

Love: an object of warm affection; a strong positive emotion of regard or affection; to get pleasure from.

Appreciation: an expression of gratitude; understanding the nature or meaning or quality or magnitude of something

90

Passion: an object of warm affection or devotion; an irrational but irresistible motive for a belief or action

80

Enthusiasm: a lively interest; a feeling of excitement

Eagerness: a positive feeling with choosing to push ahead with something

Happiness: emotions experienced when in a state of well-being

70

Positive expectation: belief about (or mental picture of) the future; the feeling something good is about to happen; wishing with confidence of fulfillment

Belief: any cognitive content held as true; a vague idea in which some confidence is placed

60

Openness: Characterized by an attitude of ready accessibility (especially about one's actions or purpose); not secretive; without obstruction to passage or view; willingness or readiness to receive

50

Hopefulness: full of hope; the feeling you have that some desire will be fulfilled; having or manifesting or inspiring hope; presaging good fortune

40

Contentment: happiness with one's situation in life

30

Boredom: the feeling of being uninterested because of frequent exposure or of something tediousness

20

Pessimism: a feeling that things will turn out badly; a general disposition to look on the dark side and to expect the worst of all things

17

Frustration: the act of hindering one's plans or efforts; being thwarted in one's efforts to attain goals

Impatience: a dislike in anything causing delay; a restless desire for change and excitement

Irritation: abnormal sensitivity to stimulation; an uncomfortable feeling in some part of the body

13

Overwhelmed: rendered powerless especially by an excessive amount or perfusion of something

10

Disappointment: feeling of dissatisfaction that results when expectations are not realized

Doubt: uncertainty about the truth or factuality of existence of something; a state of being unsure of something

7

Worry: a strong feeling of anxiety; a source of unhappiness or anxiety; disturb the peace of mind of; afflict with mental agitation or distress

Blame: attribute responsibility to; a reproach for some lapse or misdeed; an accusation that you are responsible for some lapse or misdeed

Discouragement: the expression of opposition or disapproval; the feeling of despair in the face of obstacles

5

Anger: a strong emotion or feeling that is oriented toward some real or supposed grievance; belligerence aroused by a real or supposed wrong

Revenge: action taken in return for an injury or offense; taking action for a perceived wrong

4

Hatred: a feeling of dislike so strong that it demands action

Rage: a feeling or state of intense or extreme anger

Jealousy: zealous vigilance; fearful or wary of being supplanted, especially apprehensive of the loss of another's affection. Feeling apprehensive or bitterness toward another

3

Insecurity: the anxiety you experience when you feel vulnerable or about to be hurt; the state of being subject to danger or injury

Guilt: remorse caused by feeling responsible for some offence; the state of having committed an offense

Unworthiness: the quality of being bad by virtue of lacking merit or value

2

Fear: an emotion experienced in anticipation of some specific pain or danger (usually accompanied by a desire to flee or flight); to be afraid or scared of; to be frightened

Grief: something that causes great unhappiness; intense sorrow caused by a loss of a loved one

1

Depression: a sad feeling of gloom and inadequacy

Despair: the feeling that everything is wrong and nothing will turn out well; a state in which everything seems wrong and will turn out badly

Powerlessness: being weak and feeble; the quality of lacking strength or power

0.5

Unconscious: lacking awareness and the capacity for sensory perception; occurring in the absence of awareness and thoughts; without conscious control, involuntary or unintended

I Don't Know: without conscious knowing of; the absence of awareness and thoughts

Dr. Richard A. Huntoon *Advanced Alternative Medicine Center Quantum Leap© The Emotional Scale©*

The Emotional Scale of Upgrades

Creator/Supreme Being
Joy/Knowledge/Empowerment/Freedom/Love/Appreciation
Passion
Enthusiasm/Eagerness/Happiness

Positive Expectation/Belief	→ Creator	
Optimism	→ Positive Expectation, Belief	
Hopefulness	→ Expectation, Belief	
Contentment	→ Enthusiasm, Take Action, Engaged	
Boredom	→ Enthusiasm, Eagerness	
Pessimism	→ Optimism, Positive Expectation, Belief	
Frustration	→ Ease Returning, Freedom, Appreciation	
Impatience	→ Patience, Ease Returning, Natural Flow	
Irritation	→ Soothing, Comfortable	
Overwhelmed	→ Eagerness, Enthusiasm, Powerful	
Disappointment	→ Happiness, Joy	
Doubt	→ Certainty, Creativity Returning	
Worry	→ Certainty, Relaxed,	
Discouragement	→ Encouragement, Enthusiasm, Eagerness	
Blame	**→ Forgiveness**	→Ownership, Responsibility
Anger	**→ Forgiveness**	→ Calm, Serene, Happiness
Revenge	**→ Forgiveness**	→ Ownership, Responsibility
Hatred	**→ Forgiveness**	→ Love, Appreciation, Passion
Resentful	**→ Forgiveness**	→ Passionate
Jealousy	**→ Forgiveness**	→Passionate
Rage	→ Calmness, Action in Joy, Action in Power	
Insecurity	→ Secure, Safe, Serenity, Relaxed	
Guilt	→ Innocence, Purity, Ownership	
Unworthiness	→ Worthiness, Empowered	
Fear	→ Brave, Empowered, Belief, Certainty	
Grief	→ Joy, Happiness, Enthusiasm	
Depression	→ Happiness, Eagerness, Engaged, Enthusiasm	
Despair	→ Happiness, Hopeful, Eagerness, Enthusiasm	
Powerlessness	→ Empowered, Creator, At Cause	
I Don't Know	→ Knowledge, I Choose To Know	
Unconscious	→ Consciousness, Choice, Engaged, At Cause	

Side Note

Anger, Forgiveness and Authority: An Example of How To Use the
Energy Of Emotions **Chart**

Everyone experiences anger at some time in life and few people truly understand what anger really is. Anger is a response in our body to the *perception* of being attacked or held back. It is a perfectly normal and healthy emotion only when the anger is over when the incident is over. In *The Secret*, focusing only on positive emotions is recommended. This is great if we live in a cocoon; however, most of us do not. Things happen that trigger old anger (from childhood or other previous experiences trapped in our Un-conscious mind) for different reasons.

Does feeling anger mean we will repel our desires? No. It may greatly slow our manifestations down if we hold onto the anger, but if our anger is transformed, it will have little effect. When we have a negative emotion come up, especially anger, I personally feel and have experienced the wonder of anger as a gift to remind me it is time for transformation. Instead of ignoring it (to possibly get triggered later) I recommend transforming the energy stored up into a new, more creative emotion which you can use to attract your desire.

For most emotions, transformation is a simple three-step process; identify the original time you felt this way, figure out what the emotion turns into, and decree your transformation. Anger though is a special case; it usually requires an additional step called… *forgiveness*.

For example:

I have a pattern of getting angry when people in front of me are driving below the speed limit and are oblivious to my being behind them. This is especially true if in the fast lane of the highway. To follow the three steps listed, 1) the emotion is "anger," which turns into 2) the "Creative Choice of Authority and Loving Action" returns through the process of "Forgiveness." 3) And my New State is "I forgive them for driving too slow in the fast lane of the highway, and I forgive myself for putting myself behind them. I then take my authority back and choose to go around them when it is safe to do so and I feel better taking my power back by passing them."

Appreciate that the upper right hand corner of the Energy of Emotions Chart is Love &/or Intuition Returning. This is our natural state and the one we all desire to achieve. After all, Love conquers all and Love is all there is. And I agree that as emotional beings who are affected by negative emotions, our life experience isn't always about feeling or giving love. So how do we fall out of love?

Falling Out Of Love

A story of How One drops into Un-consciousness - *To there and back again.*

All of us wonder at some point or another in our life, "*How do I get so out of balance, and what does it take to get back into harmony?*" I have looked at this question a lot in my own life, both for myself and for my practice base. The great part about it is, once you see how it occurs, it really is a simple formula to get back into alignment with your source energy. The true process of play will allow you to get back to your source. We have all sorts of examples around us, pretty much all the time. I am referring to the children in our world. I remember as a kid, as I am sure you can as well, playing all the time. Everything was a game. Everything was about having fun. When I was in early grade school, I remember playing kickball on the playground with my classmates. You could already tell the difference between those who had developed some athletic ability and those who had not. When we chose captains to pick sides, it always came down to who took the last person who was already perceived as "*the worst player.*" This only mattered because winning was the sole outcome worth "*fighting*" for.

The concept of winning and losing is an adult concept invented a long time ago. What many fail to see is that all outcomes are "*successful*" in the sense that the cycle of action is completed. A result is attained. It is considered unsuccessful only when it doesn't turn out the way we think it should have. Few things do the first time. Humans are always going to "*judge*" something based on their thought about it. I could get into the whole concept of *"right"* and *"wrong"* but that wouldn't serve the purpose of this portion of the book. There are many hundreds of books and theories related to this topic. I want to help you understand how each of us falls out of love and is Un-conscious of how we ended up that way.

Back to the best part of this childhood story. Now when playing on a team, everyone rallies around their teammates and pulls for their success. As a kid I remember a concept that is right in line with higher consciousness. The concept that we used as kids on a playground always showed up at one point or another during the game. Kickball was one of my favorite games. I remember so many times when the perfect pitch come rolling into me as the kicker, running up to meet it, and then kicking the ball as hard as I could. This was such a great feeling! To see the ball take off into the air and sail over everyone's head and into the outfield made the outcome that much better. Competition always found its way into the game. Obviously, the pitcher on one or both teams did not want that big kick to happen, so we developed the skill of pitching *"spinners."* This was kickball's version of a curve ball. The ball would come into the kicking circle spinning sideways. Frequently the ball would spin off the kicker's foot and either go foul or only a short distance. The rules of 3 strikes and you're out, and three outs and you switch sides, were in effect, so if you wanted the opportunity to kick the ball, competition between the pitchers developed. Each team found their best pitcher who threw the best spinners and the game would lose its flavor and become about winners and losers.

Right before this competitive force took hold of all of us as kids, there was a spirit of play and having fun. When those who were not as developed or blessed with athleticism put forth their best effort, and were not able to do it *"right,"* everyone playing yelled the same thing. Picture the pitch coming into the kicker, the kicker running to kick it and the ball fouling off his foot. Before the kicker could feel bad, everyone yelled *"DO OVER!"* and the person who fouled the ball off got another chance to kick. The game remained fun. Since the name of the game was *"kickball,"* it only made sense. Everyone got to kick the ball well, and everyone felt like winners. Thus the spirit of play prevailed. All was right in Our Universe, because everyone was having fun, which is the purpose of a game. More importantly, everyone was a winner because they had successfully kicked the ball.

Once it became about winners and losers, the outcome for many was not fun anymore. If you were a little behind in your development, or if you became concerned about "doing it wrong" the cycle of "*Falling out of Love*" began to develop.

If you refer to your "*Energy of Emotions*" Chart on page 31, across the top in the upper right hand corner are the words **Love and Intuition Returning**. When we are in alignment with our source energy we are love and love expressed. When we stop that motion of love, we become e-motional. The first thing that happens when we are out of alignment is pain on some level. That pain can be sensed as a little agitation or angst or simply being uncomfortable. Something is just off or not right. On the other extreme is full blown debilitating pain. This will either present itself as physical or emotional pain. Once the Un-conscious mind is in the mode of "this hurts", it drops down into the next band width known as Anger.

To arrive in the Anger band, we have to give up control. This can really be described as giving up our authority. We say things like "*They did this to me.*" "*It's their fault this happened.*" When we blame others we give up our control. We literally give away our power or energy. We feel a sense of being out of balance which will initially feel a little frustrating, but it can blossom into full blown anger or rage.

Once there, if we continue to feel that we have lost control, we begin to fall into the Fear band, where we start to doubt our abilities. We begin to lose faith, trust, security, confidence and courage in ourselves. We say "*I'm worried,*" or "*I'm scared.*" This is the fear that is so common in society today, and this is where our media resides. This is the band in which most news is delivered, and it promotes fear. Fear of being out of control and fear that we might lose it all. Stay in fear long enough and you will naturally begin to slip into the Grief band.

Having lost your faith, thoughts such as "*things never work out.*" or "*I always have to…*" lead to a loss of Joy and Happiness resulting in Grief, sadness or shame and other related emotions. Much of society in the United States feels like this. If you stay there too long, you will naturally begin to slip into the Apathy band.

Once in the Apathy band, thoughts such as, "*I can't.*" or "*It's too hard.*" result and sponsor feeling bad about yourself (low self-esteem), lack of control, and confusion.

So much of society lacks the confidence to do anything, because they lack confidence in themselves. We look to our leaders to take care of us. The result is a society, much like ours today, where no one takes responsibility for what they have created. Everyone attacks everyone else, and no one feels they have the control to do anything. People become confused as to how to help themselves feel better.

Once you reach the state of confusion, the Un-conscious mind takes over and you become Un-conscious. Not Un-conscious meaning not awake, but Un-conscious defined as a lack of conscious understanding of what is going on. You will use the famous phrase all little kids use, "*I don't know.*" or "*I don't understand.*" Once you arrive here, your life is controlling you and you don't have any sense of what to do. You lack the understanding of what to do. Please know that all of us have experienced this. Even the "*smart*" or "*together people*" experience this state. I believe that most of our country is in this state right now. The difference between being successful and being in a rut is what happens after you find yourself there.

There is a phrase, "*It is not what happens, it is what you do after it happens*". When you find yourself in an uncomfortable situation or circumstance, the first thing to do is acknowledge where you are. Admit this fact. Admit to yourself that it is your life, and because you are in this situation, you must be Un-conscious. The simple fact is that you would not purposefully put yourself behind the "eight ball." You would not have consciously chosen to have the difficult circumstances you do. Using the *Energy of Emotions* Chart will help you to determine how far down the scale you have fallen.

Initially, I always recommend starting with the Un-conscious band. This is true because if you find yourself in a place of "*How did I get here?*" then you are, by definition, Un-conscious. By claiming your state, you are now on the road to resolution. You are now conscious of and have feelings about where you are.

Once you start to tell your Un-conscious mind how you feel, initially it will move you up into the Apathy band. Here you might have some negative self-talk rise into your consciousness with phrases like "*I am such a failure;*" or "*I am no good.*" This is actually a good sign. You are right where you need to be. Recognition of this point is the first step toward restoring your balance. At this point you begin by changing your statements consciously to say things like, "*I choose to make this easy;*" or "*GOD in me can;*" or "*I choose my clarity.*"

Once you have become conscious of this, you will naturally find yourself moving up into the Grief band and you might begin to say to yourself, *"This always happens to me;"* or *"Things never work out for me."* Begin replacing those statements with new, more conscious thoughts like, *"I accept what is and I am proud of my ability to handle this."* Or *"I feel good about learning from my experience and I'm happy it happened."* Or *"I feel my joy returning."* You are gaining momentum and moving up the scale.

Next you will rise up into the Fear band and perhaps thoughts of *"I'm worried this positive feeling won't last and the problems will come back"* will surface. Replace those thoughts with upgraded thoughts of *"I have my courage to keep going and I trust things will work out and I am secure in that fact."* Once you reach this point, you are almost home. This will move you up to the Anger band.

Anger is the final band to handle. To fully handle your anger, you have to come to the realization that you did this to yourself. This is the hardest step. Taking ownership of what you created. To be in authority means you are the author. You wrote the script and are the star of your own theatrical play called *"My Life."* To take back your power, initially you will begin by forgiving the perceived wrong that was done to you. Forgive the person or circumstance which caused you to let go of your control. Forgive whatever or whomever you believe caused you to let go of your authority. This is difficult, especially if you feel the person violated you in some way. Know that as you become more conscious, there is a point where you must take full responsibility for everything that happens to you. This means everything in your life. This is the tipping point and what stops the whole dynamic of life being difficult. The phrase, *"Nothing happens to you, it all happens through you"* is appropriate for going forward once you've reached this level of consciousness. To take full responsibility means you will say (and mean), *"I am fully responsible for my experiences in my life, and I am grateful for my experiences."* At that point you will need to forgive a second time. Now you need to forgive yourself.

I say forgiveness of self needs to be done on three different levels. The first is forgiveness of yourself for allowing it to happen to you. This can be easy for some and more difficult to others. As you play with this for different aspects of your life, it certainly will become easier.

The second is forgiveness for giving up your authority in the first place and taking on the victim mentality. This is quite common in society. This is why there are so many lawsuits and arguments between people. Being responsible for your experience in life will prevent anyone from taking your power. You stay in control and then the fun begins. You don't tend to attract negative circumstances into your life anymore.

Finally, forgive yourself for having forgotten that you are the source of your experience. Therefore, you agreed to the experience you had on some level you were not conscious of. Hence, that is the reason you fell out of love with your life and yourself. This actually is the purpose of life; to experience the process of "To there and back again." After all, life is a process. Begin playing with this concept to get back to love. Once you can do this fully and completely, you will naturally feel the highest levels of emotion, those of Love, Enthusiasm and Being Creator. Then you will have truly stepped fully into your power as the conscious creator of your life experience.

Play with this concept by beginning with something easy. Do not choose a huge life pattern that is the most difficult challenge in your life. Start small and develop some transformative muscles. Use the *Energy of Emotions* chart and develop the knack of working your way up this chart. Transform all your Un-consciousness consciously. Your life will begin to change for the better. The more you practice this, the more you will return to the love and enthusiasm you had as a kid. The best part is that the next time you find one of your choices has created a less than desirable outcome, you can simply say *"Do Over!*

The Power of Forgiveness

Forgiveness is possibly the most powerful act we can use to create and possibly one of the most misunderstood. I have had many practice members say, *"How can I forgive XXX for what they did, it was so terrible?"* The answer is, forgiveness does NOT say, *"I approve of what you did, please do it again."* What it does say is, *"I take full responsibility for my life, thank you for my experiences I unknowingly asked for. I take back my authority and absolve you from any responsibility."* Once we have fully forgiven the person or the act, then, again through decreeing, we claim our authority we had given away in the original situation. If we are truly in our own power, authoring our life, then no one can do something to us (aka: we have no one or nothing to blame). By claiming and having our authority, we begin to consciously move into our personal realm of creation and attraction, because we say to Our Universe, "*I am responsible for my life and what I attract to me.*"

Authority, by the way, does NOT mean "*authoritarian.*" It is NOT about dominating others. It is about claiming our right to our space, our self, our bodies and our lives. Authority has the root "*author.*" An author is someone who writes whatever story they desire. When we are in authority in our lives, we get to write our own personal story the way we choose.

The following is an example of **How To Walk Your Way Up The Emotional Scale** using the **Energy of Emotions** Chart. It was given to me by one of my graduates of my *Quantum Leap© Seminar*.

My Father Being Controlling and Manipulative

<u>Un-conscious:</u> Over time I became numb because I just didn't understand. However, I am conscious of why he did these things. He did them to protect me from harm, although I forgive him for his lack of compassion for others feelings, my feelings.

<u>Apathy:</u> This led me to being confused and disgusted. I felt this way because I never knew who to turn to, to help me solve problems at the time I needed to solve them which lead me to being depressed because I gave up on my own life. Things began to get confusing because I didn't know where to go, which lead me to think I can't do anything to please my father, so why try to become a better person? I now see my guardian angels, whoever they may be. They are helping me along my new path and I am starting to feel better about who I am now, after looking at these lessons of why these things happened to me. I was always there to be strong for my brother, sister and mom.

<u>Grief:</u> I feel sad and mortified about facing these traumas. I feel no one should have to endure being yelled at or made fun of. This lead to wounding my pride because I felt I was under his thumb; Much like a giant Ogre type person holding down a smaller

person from escaping. I always felt bullies should see for themselves what it feels like to be bullied. They should feel the same fear they inflict on their victims. I also read in *Think & Grow Rich* these people should be put in jail. Not even a dog would put up with that much abuse before it runs away.

I accept what has happened to me only because it shows me what not to do to others and hope I see it when these feelings happen. I do feel some joy from doing this exercise because I am letting go of years of suppressed anger towards myself and for not being strong enough to defend myself from being bullied by my father.

I am now proud of my accomplishments and I am looking forward to my success.

Fear: Looking at my past I have become insecure and scared because I have become used to being held down and lost. I feel afraid of being successful as much as feeling afraid of failure. I have blamed others for these character defects. Mostly I blame myself for letting it happen. I am trusting Doc Rick Huntoon to help me clear my memories of my past and be stronger to become who I was always meant to be. I now feel confident enough to start my new business in internet marketing, and I feel many other people go through the same emotions as I. I hope to pass along my experiences, strengths and hopes so others do not feel so alone.

Anger: I have always been angry within myself for not having or developing the coping skills of dealing with my past and for seeking the help I needed. I am mad at myself for turning to drugs and alcohol to mask the pain, instead of getting educational tools to deal with life. I get irritated when I see others making the same mistakes over and over just as I have. I have become defensive towards others because instead of seeing the good advice someone may share to help me, I see them as being on the attack as I felt my father was when I was younger. I forgive my father and what I felt was his wrongdoing because I wasn't smart enough to see through the real lesson he was trying to teach me. Mostly I am angry with myself for not seeing the big picture of life.

After writing this paper, I do forgive myself for the years of resentment I held onto because I held onto the bullshit instead of learning to be me for who I am. I do forgive my father because this is probably the way he was raised as his father raised him. Although my Grandfather left his parents in Italy years before, perhaps he ran away from abuse himself, and my father ended up not wanting to see me doing the same thing and the same hardships of being alone. I now have the authority to move on because I don't have the fear anymore since he has passed on. I now have the freedom to be me. As I know I am new to this freedom, it is scary to change.

I am in control of my new life and destiny.

<u>Pain:</u> I have felt physical pain in my knees and chest. I also feel hatred towards myself for martyring myself instead of having the courage to change. The pain is over eating, eating the wrong or comfort foods and smoking cigarettes. All of which I know for a fact is harmful to me and my well being. I am changing my pain into love for myself.

I accept my intuition and new found love for myself. I surrender to my feelings of being a lost little boy and becoming the new person I am meant to be.

Thanks Doc Rick

When he sent this to me in the mail and asked me if he had done the exercise correctly, I reassured him he had done it perfectly. He then shared with me that he felt a huge weight come off his back, as he had finally taken the time to forgive his father. Although his father had died prior to taking *Quantum Leap© Seminar*, he was glad he had taken the time to go through the process. He said the forgiveness of his father and then forgiving himself was transformational. I was and am very proud of him. He took the time and went through the process to heal a problem he had been carrying with him his whole life.

Limiting Language:
How What We Speak Limits Our Beliefs

This next section is about the thoughts we have and the words we speak (out loud or to ourselves). It helps us to understand how we limit our ability to create in our lives. Please read through this section carefully and make notes of which *Limiting Language* you use. Be honest with yourself. First you will begin to discover why your life seems to be limited, and then you can consciously choose to upgrade your language. When you upgrade your language, you will begin to manifest better and more desirable outcomes.

Limiting Language: *Lack In General*

This tells our Un-conscious mind that we don't have what we choose to have. Our focus is then on "the lack," and this naturally will attract more "lack." Pay attention to the definitions of the words you use. For instance, the word "*want*" by definition means "*to desire without having, or to lack.*" If your focus is on "*wanting*," it is also (on an Un-conscious level) focused on "*lacking.*" Therefore your Un-conscious mind says, "*O.K., you lack….*" Since no one would consciously walk around stating, "*I lack…*" consider these upgrades:

I want	→ *I choose, I desire*
I need	→ *I require, I choose, I desire*

Upgrades that Focus Your Intent On Having

When we change our language to "*I choose*" or "*I desire*", we move our focus in a positive direction. "*I choose*" comes from the state of being able to choose. We are now coming from our heart. Our Un-conscious mind is now focused on what we desire to have. And then Our Universe can begin to bring it to us, as we are aligned both consciously and Un-consciously.

Limiting Language: *Lack of Consciousness*

When we tell ourselves, "*I don't know*" or "*I don't understand*", our Un-conscious mind says "*OK*" and suppresses our knowledge or ability further.

I don't know (how)	→ *I choose to know, I can know, GOD in me knows*
I can't remember	→ *I choose to remember, I will remember in a minute, I do remember*

I don't understand	→*I choose to understand, I do understand*
I'm not sure	→*I choose my surety, I am sure, I know, I remember*

Upgrades to Focus Your Intent on Choosing Consciousness

When we tell ourselves "*I choose to know*" for example, our Un-conscious mind has permission to know. How many times have you said, "*I'll remember in a minute*" and then you do, a minute later? It works because you have convinced your Un-conscious mind to do what you tell it to do. Remember, *Focusing Your Intent* with your thoughts and your words is using your words consciously to get into your *feeling* of already having what you desire.

Limiting Language: *Failed Already*

When we tell ourselves "*I can't*" or "*It's too hard,*" we set ourselves up to fail before we even begin. Our Un-conscious mind says, "*OK, you can't*" and our ability to *do* or *create* is stopped.

I can't	→ *I can, I choose to, I will myself to*
I run into a wall	→ *I am free to, I am able to, I choose to, I can*
I'm blocked (This implies something or someone is actively stopping them)	→ *xxx chooses for me to, I can, I choose to, I am free to*
I'm numb (indicates being Un-conscious of something)	→ *I feel (my situation), I choose to feel, I am aware of*
It's beyond my control	→ *I'm in control of, I can, I am able to*
If all else fails then…	(If we plan for failure, we may get it. Don't leave a back door.) → *I will succeed, I can, xxx will work/succeed*
It's too hard	→ *It's easy for me, I can, It's possible to*

Upgrades to Focus Your Intent on Having Possibility

When we tell ourselves "*I can*" or "*I choose to*" in a situation in which we have *ease returning to us*, we allow room for our Un-conscious mind to help us see a new possibility for our situation. Basically, "*Say you can and you can.*"

Limiting Language: *Struggle*

When we tell ourselves *"It's hard"* we set ourselves up to have difficulty in a given situation. There is a difference between *"It's too hard"* and *"It's hard"*. *"It's too hard"* speaks of failure. *"It's hard"* speaks about difficulty. When we say *"It's difficult."* our Un-conscious mind says, *"OK, let's have struggle and difficulty."*

It's hard	→ **I have ease returning, I choose to make it easy**
I'm struggling	→ **I choose my easy life, This is easy for me**
Striving for	→ **I have, I can, I am, It is**

Upgrades to Focus Your Intent on Ease

Saying *"I have ease returning to me."* or *"I choose to make this easy."* feels much different than *"It's hard."* *"Ease returning"* allows for movement, for possibility and for creativity. It opens you up. Remember, change your feeling, change your intent, and change your experience!

Limiting Language: *Starting From Doubt & Guilt*

These all have the energy of "*I can't*" or "*I won't.*" "*I can't*" leads to self-doubt, which often leads to wishy-washy (technical term) language. When someone tells you, "*I'll try.*" you know from the start it will probably never happen.

I should do...	→ **I choose to, I am doing it**
I hope I...	→ **I will, I can**
I would but	→**No, Yes (choose one and commit to it)**
I need to	→ **I choose to**

I might	→ *I will, I won't, I can*
I wish	→ *I have, I can*
I'll try	→ *I will, I won't, I can (choose one and commit)*
I have to	→ *I choose to, I am doing it*

Upgrades to Specific Action/Intention

This is a very simple upgrade. State your intent clearly when talking to people. If you choose to do something, just do it. If you are not willing to commit to something, say "*No.*" If you are willing, say "*Yes.*" Remember what Yoda said: "*Do or do not. There is no try.*"

Limiting Language: *Non-Sense/Not Willing To Commit*

A phrase like "*isn't it?*" mean literally "*is not it?*" This phrase essentially says nothing, and is non-sense. As a result the Un-conscious is confused and basically creates nothing. Pay attention to contractions, and what you are actually saying with them. Often, these phrases are used in an attempt to get others to agree, or to make requests in a non-committal way.

Isn't it a beautiful day?	→ *I'm enjoying my lovely day. It is a lovely day.*
Wouldn't you	→ *Will you?*
Shouldn't you	→ *I recommend you... I invite you to... I encourage*
Couldn't you	→ *Can you? Will you?*
Haven't they	→ *Have they?*
Doesn't it	→ *Does it?*
Can't you	→ *Can you? Will You?*

Limiting Language: *Lack of Commitment*

The following examples are additional ways to avoid committing to something. Every one of these choices is about a lack of commitment (committing to yourself and your choices).

I kind of (kinda) want	→ *I desire, I choose, I require*
Sort of (Sorta)	→ *Yes, No*
I probably will go	→ *I will go, I won't go, I will check my calendar*
Well, maybe	→ *Yes, No*
Perhaps	→ *Yes, No*
Could be	→ *Yes, No*
Possibly, I could	→ *I will, I won't*
I'll try to	→ *I will, I won't*
I intend to	→ *I will, I won't*
Attempt to	→ *I will, I won't*
Would like to	→ *I will, I won't*
I'm ready to	→ *I will, I won't*

Both Non-Sense and Lacking Commitment Upgrade to Focus Your Intent to Have Clarity, Take Responsibility, Commit and Take Action

Say what you mean and mean what you say. This is one way to keep your agreement to "*Live Your Word.*" Start with your choices. **YOU make YOUR choices, then commit to yourself, AND THEN commit to others.** When you choose and then commit, your Un-conscious and conscious will be aligned to attract the results you desire.

When someone starts a sentence with, "*Well,*" you can bet on a non-committal sentence.

Consider the following:

"*Until one is committed there is hesitancy, the chance of drawback, and always ineffectiveness. There is one Elementary Truth concerning all acts of initiative (and creation), the ignorance of which kills countless ideas and splendid plans: the moment one commits oneself to totally, is the one providence moves too.*

All sorts of things occur to help create that which would otherwise never have occurred. A whole stream of events issues from the decision, rising in one's favor all manner of unforeseen incidents and meetings and material assistance, which no man could have dreamt would come his way."

W. N. Murray – The Scottish Himalayan Expedition 1951

If you leave yourself a back door, or a way out, your focus will be divided between moving forward towards your desire and a way out or failure. What we focus on is what we attract. If our focus is divided between forward and backward, what we will attract is "*stuck*". A commitment has no back door, no way out. Forward is our only possibility. Success is our only option.

Limiting Language: *Focus On What We DON'T Desire*

This category is all about focus. *The Law of Attraction* is about attracting what we desire. When we talk about exactly what we are trying to get rid of in our lives our focus goes there. If a person running the high hurdles looks at (focuses on) the hurdles, he tends to hit them. This is why runners are trained to look where they choose to go, above the hurdles. This is an apt metaphor. *When we focus on our personal hurdles and what we do NOT desire, we attract more of those undesired outcomes.*

I choose to, I will…	→ **I choose, I am, I am being**
…not be …not have	→ **I choose to have or be the (opposite of)**
…not do	→ **I choose to do (opposite of)**
	e.g. *I choose to not go to the movies. Upgrades to I choose to stay home.*
…lose (weight, etc.)	→ **I am thin, I have my firm body, I have my strong body**
…stop or quit	→ **I choose my healthy lungs, I only eat healthy foods**
	e.g. smoking, eating junk, drinking, etc.
…I don't want	→ **I choose (what you choose to have)**
…I'd like to get rid of	→ **I have (opposite of)**

<u>Upgrades to Stating Only What We Desire</u>

Upgrading this category requires knowing what you DO choose to have. Why are you choosing to quit smoking??? Is it to save money? Is it to live longer? Is it to smell better? Is it to have healthy lungs? Check in with your *Inner Guidance* and know WHY you desire to quit or stop and focus ONLY on what your true desire really is. What is your benefit? Focus there.

Limiting Language: *Language of Separation*

Being vague with our intention actually separates us in consciousness from what we truly desire. If we say, "*I choose a nice car*", our Un-conscious mind doesn't know WHOSE nice car, so we may just attract a new neighbor with a Ferrari. Here we are not connecting specifically with what we desire. In addition, "*a nice car*" really doesn't evoke much emotion. Now, "*I choose my new shinny, red Ferrari.*" does. "*My car*" also connects us to what we desire, with feeling, thus bringing it to us faster.

The car	→ *My car, Your car, Their car, Our car etc.*
This book	→ *My, Yours, Our, Their, His, Her*
These gifts	→ *My, Yours, Our, Their, His, Her*
The money	→ *My, Yours, Our, Their, His, Her*
That chair	→ *My, Yours, Our, Their, His, Her*
A new bike	→ *My, Yours, Our, Their, His, Her*
Those friends	→ *My, Yours, Our, Their, His, Her*
The shoulder	→ *My, Yours, Our, Their, His, Her*
This life	→ *My, Yours, Our, Their, His, Her*
I feel that I love them	→ *I love them*
The choices I make	→ *My choices*
It feels good when I	→ *I feel good when I*
You know when you…	→ *When I xxx then I yyy*

Upgrades To Ownership/Specificity

If you desire something, then own what you desire, describe it with specificity and you will attract it much faster. PLEASE remember that these are NOT absolutes. Have some flexibility. If you are pointing to a chair in a store, there is nothing wrong with saying "that chair." The "T" words can both separate as well as connect two things. Be aware of which you are speaking. *That, Those, These, They, Them, It,* and *The* will slow communication in the Un-conscious, since the Un-conscious needs to figure out what each "T" word refers to before going on.

Limiting Language: *Choice with Conditions*

If we say, "*I choose my new job in order to have more money,*" we are placing a condition on what we choose to attract. *The Law of Attraction* says: 1) Ask - 2) Our Universe Answers - 3) Receive (Ask & It Is Given, *Hicks*). This means stay out of the HOW in Step 2. If we tell *Our Universe* that the only way we will attract more money is to have a new job, then what you are really telling *Your Universe* is, "*I don't really trust you, so I will tell you how to give me what I desire.*"

Another way to put conditions on our creation is to say. "*I will go there so that I will feel accepted.*" What we are saying is that we will ONLY feel accepted when we go there. If we desire acceptance, then just BE accepted. We can decree "*I feel accepted and I enjoy going there,*" and our acceptance no longer has a condition tied to it.

I choose my new job in order to have more money

       → **I have my millions & I have my new job.**

I go there so that I will feel accepted → **I feel accepted & I enjoy going there**

When I have this…then I will   → **I will….**

If… then….   → **I will…**

I choose my new house because then….. → **I choose my new house.**

Upgrades to Focus Your Intent by Committing To What You Choose

In *The Secret* many of the speakers talked about imagining your desires have already been fulfilled as a powerful way to get into your feelings of having. This is why it is important to upgrade "*Choice with Conditions.*" Using "*Choice with Conditions*" separates you from your feeling of already having something. Make your choice (state a desire) that stands on its own and feel as though you already have it and you will begin to attract it to you.

Limiting Language: *Absolutes*

Again, attraction follows feeling and feeling follows specificity. Absolute and grandiose phrases tell our Un-conscious to send out a thousand ripe tomatoes and hope one hits the target. Look at the first example: "*So everyone will love me.*" We don't know everyone. There may be six degrees of separation between us and Kevin Bacon, yet we still don't know him or really care if he loves us or not. What we really desire is love from and with our parents, our children, our divine partners, and the like.

So everyone will love me	→ *I choose for my mom and dad to love me*
I always pick the wrong one	→ *In the past I picked the wrong relationships, and now I choose to have my loving partner*
Everything I have always wanted	→ *I have (something specific)*
My complete transformation	→ *I am now, I will (specifics)*
I'll improve	→ *I am...*
Absolutely	→ *Yes, No*
The best	→ *I am very good at*
My all	→ *I did (specifics)*

Upgrades to Focus Your Intent with Specificity & Creativity

Your upgrade here is to find what you really desire. Your *Inner Guidance* will help you with this). Get specific with: *who, what, when, for how long, how much, how often, color, size, taste, feel, temperature, taste,* and *sound.* Then decree with specificity what you desire.

Limiting Language: *Co-Dependent & Lack Of Authority*

These all speak from a victim's viewpoint. We are either victims or creators, period. There is no middle ground. If we talk around being a victim we will attract more reasons to be a victim. We give away our creative power to something outside of our self. Being a creator means we have both responsibility for our life, AND authorship of our life. When we are attracting what we desire, we are our own author.

I must…	→ *I choose to…, I will it so*
I have to…	→ *I choose to…, I will…*
I had to…	→ *I did it, I chose to*
I've got to…	→ *I will*
They made me	→ *Rather than accept the consequences, I chose to*
I feel like	→ *I feel angry (sad, upset, etc.)*
Let me…	→ *I require a few minutes to think about it, I'm going to the restroom*
You make me feel (happy, sad, etc)	→ *I am happy; I am my own source of happiness*
It's their fault that…	→ *I accept full responsibility for…*

Upgrades to Focus Your Intent with Co-Empowerment & Authority/ Responsibility

These are very easy to upgrade in language. Taking your authority in consciousness is the important aspect. "*I will…*" (*use your will,* and not put your choices off in the future) is often a powerful statement of authority. Then your Un-conscious mind pays attention and sets up situations where you attract what you choose. Co-empowerment literally means, "*I am responsible for my own xxx (happiness, success, authority, anger)*".

Limiting Language: *I Didn't Really Mean It*

When we connect two phrases with the words "*but*", "*however*", "*although*", and "*yet*", what is being communicated is we don't really mean the first phrase. "*Honey, did you like the dinner I prepared?*" "*Yes, but, the chicken was a little overdone.*" The "*but*" cancels out the intent preceding it.

I love you, but I require... → **I love you and I require you treat me with respect**

I really want to be there for you, however...
→ **I am busy at the time.**

You did a great job, although...
→ **Thank you. I would like you to do it this way in the future.**

Upgrades to Mean What You Say

Have your courage to say what you mean in the first place. "*And*" can be a great connector when you really mean both phrases in a compound sentence.

Limiting Language: *In Process*

This is not necessarily a limiting state AND it is upgradeable. Change and transformation can be the beginning of being more conscious. Process is often the beginning of some people saving their lives. When someone is stuck, or constantly in process, they are often avoiding real change. More importantly, staying in process is a way to avoid their outcome - usually for Un-conscious reasons. You've heard this before: "*I'm working on changing my...*" and the next month they are still "*working on it*".

....changing it	→ *I have, I am, I love*
....differently	→ *I now do it....*
....transforming it	→ *I have, I am, I love, I enjoy*
I'm getting more healthy	→ *I am healthy everyday*
....dealing with it	→ *I have, I am, I love*
....working on it	→ *I have, I am, I love*
....healing it	→ *I am healthy, I have my healthy...*
I am choosing....	→ *I have, I am, I love*
I am trying to...	→ *I am doing, I am*
I am in the process of...	→ *I am doing, I am*

Upgrade to Completion

This is a subtle and powerful upgrade, and it requires a "*leap of faith*" to use. For this upgrade to "*work*" you must understand the fact that you only have "*now*". There is no tomorrow in reality. Your Un-conscious mind only knows "*now*". So, when you tell your Un-conscious mind you are changing something, you're Un-conscious mind says, "*OK*" and attracts more things to change. The upgrade then is to speak to being already IN your desired state. Instead of healing our bodies, be healed now. I even prefer to go to "*I am healthy now*", because if we are focused on being healed, we must have something to heal.

I have heard objections to doing this from people who say: "*It is a lie if I say I am healed when I have this terrible disease.*" I always offer the following. Since we only have now, it is truth. It must become true in our Un-conscious & conscious mind BEFORE it will be true in our outside reality. Physical change occurs after we are congruent with it both in our conscious and Un-conscious mind. Therefore, speak as if it is true. You will get you into the feeling of having it, and *The Law of Attraction* can then bring it to you.

Focusing Language That Moves You Toward Your Outcome Fulfilled

This is the start of active, creative language, and it still uses many "*In Process*" phrases and language. Examples:

I come from having....

I empower myself to have....

I claim....

I imagine having....

I give myself permission to....

I choose to....

Note: Some people get stuck in the process of moving towards having their desires fulfilled. This can be a good place to be if your life was all negative before. Just remember, you can either be in process or have your desires now....it's your choice. Process is a good place to start. It is NOT a place to stay.

Coming From Our Outcome Fulfilled

Note: In *The Secret* many of the speakers talked about imagining your desires having been fulfilled as a powerful way to instill your feelings of having. In addition, speaking with feeling (*decreeing*) as if you already have what you desire is a POWERFUL way to manifest and attract it. In this state you *Focus Your Intent*, and thus your *feelings*, on what you are *having, doing, being,* and *feeling* now that you have your desire.

Examples:

I enjoy riding in my new Ferrari, and feeling the wind in my hair.

I create my ideal relationship with my loving partner.

I love hearing the sound of the ocean in my bedroom.

I have my ideal job and I love the feeling of serving others.

I choose my destiny in life by living consciously.

I will have my millions in the bank when I choose to retire.

I can manifest my heart's desire in everything I choose.

I am very grateful for my loving family.

At the beginning of each example above are two declaratives (I enjoy, I create, etc.) which help to focus the energy of creation within you. Each two word phrase correlates to an Energy Center within your body. These Energy Centers are known as Chakras, derived from Sanskrit and are used widely in the practice of *Yoga* as well as *meditation*. Chakras are any of the points of spiritual power located within the body, usually given as seven in number. The points are personified by gods and can be released through the proper exercises. These will be given as a tool later in the book, Tool Box Item # 12. (See diagram page 133)

When you take the time to focus energy using these specific two word phrases (declaratives) and combine your intention by focusing your energy in each of your corresponding Energy Centers, you help to increase the strength of creation within each Center and also within you.

Using *I Am, I Can, I Will etc.* at the beginning of sentences will create specific focus in each of your 7 main Energy Centers (Chakras) and allow you to activate your own process of creation. See the following chart for help with this.

Focusing Language

Example Phrases For Coming From Your Outcome Fulfilled

Declarative Energy Center Body Location Meaning of each Center

Declarative	Energy Center	Body Location	Meaning of each Center
I Am	Root Chakra	Base of Spine	Our beginning of Consciousness, Our Foundation
I Can	Pelvic Chakra	Below Belly	Our beginning of Recognizing Our ability to do

I Will	Self Chakra	Below Sternum	Our beginning of Ownership and Responsibility
I Choose	Heart Chakra	Center of Chest	Our beginning to Choose our outcomes with Love
I Have	Throat Chakra	Center of Throat	Our beginning of Authority and Authorship
I Love	Third Eye Chakra	Center of Brow	Our beginning of Recognizing we ARE love
I Create	Crown Chakra	Top of the Head	We are the Creator and we know who we are
I Enjoy	Transpersonal	Above The Head	Our connection to our divine self/Our true purpose

Play with this yourself to practice developing conscious focus on what you truly desire to experience in your life. The deeper you can get into your *feeling* of *having*, *doing* and *being* it, the faster *Your Universe* will bring it to you.

Tool Box Item # 2
Observe The Moment

This technique is used anytime you find yourself in a situation or circumstance where you are aware that you are upset and emotional. Since we know that emotion is moving away from your center or your true self, this is a quick and easy way to snap out of it, since it allows you to choose your state of being.

Observe The Moment: Focus on and speak about what you see directly in front of your face right NOW and describe it with every sense you can. What you observe to be true NOW: colors, shapes, textures, temperature, sounds, smell, and even taste if it is appropriate. Observe it, as it exists NOW, **_WITHOUT_** emotion, interpretation or explanation about why you think it is so. Resist all justifications for what you are observing NOW and simply observe the moment for what is true and real in front of you.

There are three realities that exist:

ULTIMATE REALITY
FACTUAL REALITY
DISTORTED REALITY

Two of the THREE REALITIES we deal with every day. Which of the two do you spend more time with?

DISTORTED REALITY	FACTUAL REALITY
What we think is happening	What is observed and is so - factually
How we feel about what we see	What can be touched and sensed
Causes us to Re-Act	Creates a Response to what is so
Being the Result of what is so	Being the Creator of what is so
Creates Un-consciousness	Allows for Consciousness
Being Un-Present (past or future)	Being Present

Being Conscious and going without *Pasteurizing* or *Futurizing* your life in this NOW moment will allow you to focus on the only moment you have, NOW! Taking the time to focus on what is true in this NOW moment creatively makes all the difference between being happy and being un-happy. You control how you feel. The quickest way to get rid of a negative feeling is to fully identify what is true in the moment. Do this by observing and being focused on what is factually occurring, what I call *Factual Reality*. When you find yourself feeling less than happy or healthy, you have been spending time in your *Distorted Reality*. You can stay there if you choose, and you can step out of it any time you desire. The choice is yours. *Observe Your Moment!* Identify with what is by identifying what you see in front of you, with no interpretation. The choice you have is 1) allow emotions and thoughts about what you think you see from past experience and interpretation resulting in your *Distorted Reality*; OR 2) <u>consciously choose your response to what you see and go forward based on what is observed in</u> *Factual Reality*, <u>not your initial thought about it.</u>

Many times it is hard to allow ourselves to be in the moment. Since most of what grabs our attention is filtered through our Un-conscious mind, we are always comparing past to present. When it is difficult to let go of what is so strongly grounded in our Un-conscious mind (and asking for our attention through the *Law of Attraction*), it becomes important to be able to release it in order to focus on a different thought. Think of it like being on a trapeze. If you swing from one to the other, you have to let go of the first bar in order to grab the second bar.

The following tool is all about releasing. It is given to you here in an effort to create the space for newness and change. If you choose to park your car in a spot that is occupied by another car, the first car must vacate the spot before you can move in there. Your Un-conscious mind is no different. If your life is going to change for the better, it is important for you to release what you do not want anymore and replace it with something you choose for yourself. Therefore, releasing is the first step towards change, after finding out where you are and determining where you choose to go.

The following is a simple 5 step process used to release anything. It was adapted from Hale Dwoskin's *Sedona Method*. It is a very powerful and simple tool to use. Once you become familiar with it, you can release anything in a fraction of a second. Have fun with it.

<u>Toolbox Item # 3</u>
<u>Releasing</u>

1. What is the most NOW feeling within your body (it could be physical, or emotional) that you are not happy with?
2. Could you welcome that feeling fully into your body and allow yourself to feel it 100 %? (what I do is visualize that feeling in my hands and squeeze it as tight as I can)
3. Could you let go of that feeling?

4. Would you let go of that feeling?

5. When?

If you said **YES** to the 3rd and 4th questions, and choose to do it **NOW**, then simply release the feeling by breathing through it until you are lighter and sense the feeling is gone. Your hands will gradually open as you release the feeling until it is gone.

At this point, you check in with yourself and see if the original feeling is fully gone.

Repeat the process if necessary until you almost feel like laughing or simply feel serene and at peace.

Some tips to help with this:

Give yourself permission to let go of only a part of it, if you can't let go of all of it at once.

If you find you have *Resistance* to letting your original feeling/emotion go, ask yourself to fully feel the Resistance and then do the 5 steps for your Resistance. Once your Resistance is gone, then return to your original feeling/emotion and do the 5 steps and release it. It is O.K. for you to release as much or as little as you choose.

Having released what we do not want, now it is important to replace it with what you do choose. The most powerful way to do that is through this next tool. Your Un-conscious mind has a belief system. As we will soon discover, it is based only on what it believes to be true. One of the easiest and most powerful ways to change a belief is to start declaring your new truth. This is done using decrees.

The following tool is all about decrees. Take the time to realize how powerful these are. Remember, the ability to speak from your heart center with certainty is what makes your decree so powerful. The more powerful your decree, the stronger the belief will become in your Un-conscious mind. Replacing old programmed beliefs with new and improved upgrades of what feels right for you is a powerful way to reprogram your Un-conscious mind, consciously. Have fun with this next tool.

Toolbox Item # 4
Decrees

A "Decree" is a statement of law, or fact, without dispute.

Using Decrees with Focusing Language will move you from neutral, or being O.K. with what is, to *Creative Choice* where you consciously choose what you desire.

Decrees, stated with feeling, convince our Un-conscious mind of the new "*fact*" which replaces the old thought pattern, or limiting belief within our Un-conscious mind.

Some people say decrees are a command sent to the "unseen" help that surrounds us.

Decree while feeling your outcome already fulfilled! *"Fake it 'til you make it."*

It is important to understand every word that you are decreeing.

Read carefully through the Decree Instructions below. This is a POWERFUL tool.

Decree Instructions

A Decree is a statement of law, or fact, without dispute. There are several opinions about why they work. One is that we convince our Un-conscious mind that what we decree is true so we will easily attract our new stated belief. Another is that we are telling our guides or angels what we command to be in existence. Whichever you believe, the instructions for using decrees are exactly the same: feel what you are commanding as if it were true NOW.

In using decrees, we have 3 all powerful pronouns to use in reference to ourselves. Each of them has a different significance.

ME – refers to our Un-conscious self

MYSELF – refers to our thinking, conscious self

I – refers to our **Eternal Self**

So, if we are using decrees to convince our Un-conscious self that we love ourselves, "*I love myself*" can be upgraded to "*I love me.*" If we are crafting a decree for ourselves when we are "stuck" in our head and unable to feel, "*I allow myself to feel me*" is a very powerful decree. It touches all 3 levels of consciousness.

Remember, **feeling is critical**. Feeling is what drives our creations. From the I Am Discourses: "*If you will read the decrees slowly and with deep, deep feeling in each word as you come to it, you will have instantaneous manifestations when you can feel the meaning in each word deeply enough.*" From the book *The Divine Matrix* by Gregg Braden, "*Feeling is the language that 'speaks' to the Divine Matrix. Feel as though your goal is accomplished and your prayer is already answered.*" And, "*Not just any feeling will do. The ones that create must be without ego or judgment.*"

Next we have an important part of our words. It is to truly understand what we are saying. This leads us to

What Does Every Word REALLY Mean?

It is important to understand EVERY word we are decreeing. The most common and powerful example is the word "*love*". If I decree, "*I love myself*", the next question is: What **IS** love? If we don't have a clear, precise definition, then our decree will have little meaning. It is even important to understand the meaning of the word "I". So, before I decree, I look up the meaning in both a dictionary and a thesaurus to really understand what I am decreeing. Then I can truly understand what I am choosing to create in my life, and more importantly, I can begin to lay down the neural pathway to foster new and clear outcomes with my decree.

WARNING

When we decree effectively, things in our lives start moving fast. If we decree a new state for our self which contradicts a deep seated belief, situations may come up which highlight our old (unwanted) belief. This allows us to transform it. Transforming it then allows our new desire to manifest.

For example; if someone desires having their millions of dollars NOW and decrees "*I have my 2.5 million dollars in my Bank of America checking account NOW!*", and they still have a belief that money creates trouble, they could manifest an audit by the IRS. If they take this as their opportunity to identify an unwanted belief and love their audit and transform the old belief into "*having money is easy and fun,*" they can then start attracting their 2.5 million dollars.

Another example is if the same person decrees having 2.5 million dollars, yet they are working 40 hours a week for $6.50 per hour, they may have to lose their job to get them to move into another profession where they can attract their millions. Again, if they just get angry and upset, they could suppress the old belief again and turn away their opportunity to have their 2.5 million dollars. Look for your blessings in every "*crisis*" and choose to make it fun, fast and easy.

STOP

Before you can have what you desire you MUST first know what it is you truly desire.

- It is RARELY money, fast cars, fast women, boats, mansions, or the like.
- It is OFTEN love with parents, love with children, security in life, faith in one's self, acceptance, nurturing, and deep spiritual connection.

If you follow your *Internal Guidance System* (some call it "*heart*", "*eternal self*" or "*intuition*"), then you are more likely to find out what your heart's true desire really is. If you seek your heart's true desire first, then all your other desires will come to you.

- Now it is helpful to ask yourself, what is the outcome of having your specific desire?
- Your outcome will often lead you to what your *Internal Guidance System* is telling you is your true desire.

I cannot emphasize enough the power of Decrees. Taking the time to do your decrees in front of a mirror or with a partner who does their decrees with you is a powerful way to change your Un-conscious core beliefs, even if you do not know what they are. By inserting a new belief with passion and enthusiasm you will allow the new belief to supersede the old outdated one. Remember - the old one can resurface under stressful circumstances if it is not fully replaced with the new one. Therefore, Decree, Decree, Decree!

Exercise # 2
Decrees

Can be practiced with a Partner or in front of a mirror
Use Your Road Map (pg. 5)
Use Energy of Emotions Chart (pg. 31)
and Examples of Focusing Language (pg. 57)
Create a New Decree (pg. 63)

Have your partner state their Decree with feeling until both of you feel they have got it (the moment they "get it" you will both notice a change in your feeling state).

Switch Partners

Having learned about and practiced using decrees, now it is time to go back to where you started from and finish Exercise # 1. By finishing this exercise, you will begin to re-program your Un-conscious mind. Certainly there will be several upgrades and re-programs to take place, and this is definitely a strong beginning. Take the time to upgrade Exercise # 1 by completing Exercise # 3.

Exercise # 3
Upgrading Exercise # 1

Step 1 - Please review the topic you wrote in Exercise # 1 and highlight or mark all limiting words and phrases (Page 17)
Step 2 - Pick ONE highlighted item and write it in the space below. Determine which category of Limiting Language it fits. Write the specific effect FOR YOU of using the Limiting Language (how has using this language limited you), and upgrade your word or phrase into your CREATIVE CHOICE, COMING FROM YOUR OUTCOME FULFILLED.

Before beginning this exercise, there are several things I recommend you keep in mind:

REMEMBER:
Be specific
Be focused on having your desired outcome
Use first person personal (make it about you)
Feel your new choices as you write them
Admit your true desires to yourself
Get aligned with each of your new choices
And when you finish...Decree, Decree, and Decree

Limiting word or phrase: _____

_____

_____

_____

Category of Limiting Language belongs in: _____

_____

What are the effects of using this Limiting Language IN YOUR LIFE? BE SPECIFIC:

_____

_____

_____

_____

_____

_____

_____

_____

_____

_____

_____

Write your NEW, UPGRADED CONSCIOUS CHOICE on your Topic Sheet pg. 16

_____

_____

_____

_____

Example of Exercise # 3

Upgrading Exercise # 1

Step 1 - Please review the topic you wrote in Exercise # 1 and highlight or mark all limiting words and phrases

Step 2 - Pick ONE highlighted item and write it in the space below. Pick the one that makes you feel most uncomfortable, or seems to bother you most. This is the one you are the most affected by. Determine which category of Limiting Language it fits into. Write the specific effect FOR YOU of using the Limiting Language (meaning how has using your language limited you), and upgrade your word or phrase into your CREATIVE CHOICE, COMING FROM YOUR OUTCOME FULFILLED.

REMEMBER:

Be specific

Be focused on having your desired outcome

Use first person personal (make it about you)

Feel your new choices as you write them

Admit to yourself your true desires

Get aligned with each of your new choices

And when you get done...Decree, Decree, and Decree

Below is an example:

Limiting word or phrase: <u>Getting Worse</u>

_____

_____

_____

_____

Category of Limiting Language belongs in: _Failed Already OR Struggle_

What are the effects of using this Limiting Language IN YOUR LIFE? BE SPECIFIC: _Limits my ability to feel good and feel good about myself. Makes me feel like I am limited and I have no ability to get better. I feel somewhat hopeless and this causes me to not want to do anything because it makes my body feel worse when I do. As a result, my life is not enjoyable and I limit my activities and willingness to engage my life. I am depressed and feel hopeless about my future._

Write your NEW, UPGRADED CONSCIOUS CHOICE on your Topic Sheet pg. 16 _My Health Is Getting Better Every Day; I Am Healthy and Strong_

Now that you have discovered your new decree, it is important to practice saying this decree over and over again. You can do this in your head when speaking it out loud is inappropriate, AND it is better for you to speak it out loud with feeling to command your Un-conscious mind to begin replacing your old limited belief, such as _Failed Already or Struggle_ from this past example. As this is new for you, I am sure you may not feel comfortable initially while doing this. And if you can get into the _spirit of play_ and embrace the power of this exercise, you can begin to re-program your Negative Core Beliefs into positive ones.

Putting It All Together- How Your Language Affects Your Day/Life

When you begin to become more conscious of the words you use and the meanings behind what you say, it doesn't take much to understand why your life is the way it is. The degree to which you speak with _Limiting Language_, will directly impact what _The Law of Attraction_ brings you. If you are not in agreement with what your life has brought you thus far, become more conscious of your words. Appreciate that everything and everyone in your life is an external clue and reflection of what you are attracting. Your internal feelings and the way you express them through your actions and words will create the life you experience. Change your way of expressing yourself by upgrading your language, and you will change your life pretty quickly. The challenge is to use the tools and exercises contained in this book to transform your Old Belief System into a new Consciously Positive Belief System.

This next tool is one you may not value initially. This is only because the information can be overwhelming. My advice to you is to read through the material and begin noticing things about yourself. Take the time to apply the information to yourself a little at a time. This may take several weeks or even months. I have been using this information for a couple of years, and I am still learning and discovering deeper understandings about myself because of it. Play with the ideas and concepts and over time they will become second nature to you. Once you see it within yourself, noticing body language in others will be easier. This really is a great tool, and when you can begin to interpret body language within yourself and others, your relationships will improve dramatically. Knowing what you are trying to say and knowing what others are trying to say (or not say) helps to create clarity in your life. And with clarity comes balance.

Toolbox Item # 5
Sacred Body Language

This tool is very valuable when taking the time to notice what is going on in the moment. You can always apply this to yourself, and many times it will help you to understand what is going on in the people you are talking to. As your consciousness increases, so will your recognition of what is really going on in yourself and others. Practice, practice, practice. Remember, the people in your life are an attractive reflection of yourself. Therefore, be mindful that everyone and every situation in your life is a reflection of you, your vibration, and where you are currently. You can change what you do not like, only after you change your vibration.

Our physical form is based on our thoughts, words and emotional patterns - the way we store and re-act to our present, based upon our past survival experiences. Symptoms are a manifestation indicating that you went off course from our I AM that I AM. You are being asked to PAY MORE ATTENTION to the area of your symptom or pain. This is an effort to put you back on course - back into harmony with yourself as a whole. Body language tells us what aspect of our self is asking for attention by expressing a symptom or pain. Therefore, we would benefit by paying attention to what the symptom represents. This means dealing with the imbalance directly, rather than finding something that will simply suppress (medication) or eliminate the symptom from our awareness. Symptoms, when dealt with directly, turn into strengths, therefore, symptoms should be acknowledged as *something returning:* i.e. Courage, Joy, Authority, Happiness. And wouldn't you feel better having more of that?

To get into the habit of dealing directly with your symptoms, ask yourself the following questions:

What is returning?

What does this symptom represent for me; and what does it turn into?

What is my body asking of me that I would benefit from paying attention to?

Ask these questions for additional help:

What is my goal?

What is keeping me from my outcome?

What change that would benefit my life am I resistant to embracing?

Answering those questions and determining what your body is asking of you will be important to bringing yourself back into alignment with your higher self.

This next section discusses what is termed *Sacred Body Language Translations.* There are thousands of years of survival techniques that humans have learned. Understanding what they mean and knowing they are hardwired into our Un-conscious minds allows us to get a glimpse into our Un-conscious minds. Being able to "see" what is there helps determine what needs to be reprogrammed and updated. This is based upon and expressed through our body language. Our bodies are always revealing to us and to the world what is going on inside our minds. It is always accurate. It simply requires spending time and learning for yourself what your body is communicating from your

Un-conscious. Study this section and practice by observing yourself first, followed by observing others to increase your awareness. Remember, observation does NOT mean judgment. Unless the person you are observing is asking for input from you, be careful not to put your observations on them.

There are whole courses on this material; the best one I know of is by a gentleman named *Robert Tennyson Stevens* who teaches a course called *Sacred Body Language Translations*. Much of what follows is taken from his work and adapted for this section. For more information about *Robert Tennyson Stevens* and his *Sacred Body Language Translations*, go to www.masterysystems.com.

Sacred Body Language Translations

Each part of your body represents a different aspect of what is going on in both your Conscious and Un-conscious mind. What we are conscious of isn't hard to interpret. Our Un-conscious is a completely different story. Knowing how to read the signs and symptoms will help you confront your Un-conscious mind and come to final resolution of your issues. Take the time to learn what each part of your body means and you will be able to handle your issues in a more timely fashion. Once you have mastered that, you will be able to help facilitate others.

HEAD: Represents THINKING, KNOWING, REMEMBERING.

NECK: Connects the HEAD and the TORSO.

NECK PAIN: Represents CONFLICT between what you are THINKING and what you are DOING. If there is neck pain, ask yourself the following:

Is there something I am THINKING that I don't want to DO? -OR-

Is there something I am DOING that I don't want to acKNOWledge?

TORSO (include arms): Represents DOING.

WAIST/HIPS: Connect the TORSO and the LEGS.

HIP PAIN: Represents a CONFLICT between what you choose to DO and actually MOVING FORWARD with it. If there is pain, ask yourself the following:

Right Hip: Is there something I am trying to DO and am having trouble MOVING FORWARD with in my life? —OR-

Left Hip: Is there something I am having difficulty WALKING AWAY FROM in my life?

LEGS/HIPS: Represent MOVING FORWARD on the Right and MOVING AWAY FROM on the left.

ANKLES/FEET: Represent standing under yourself and flexibility with understanding; Stepping into something new on the right −OR− stepping away from something old on the left.

Front Body Language Basics

The following body parts represent different aspects of our mental and emotional selves. Understand how the following body parts correspond to the different aspects of life. Many times, conditions related to the different areas will help you begin to uncover your Un-conscious thoughts. Bringing those to the surface will help you transform them into something conscious and agreeable. As you think about each one, you will begin to see the correlation.

Head: Thinking, Remembering, Conceiving, Understanding → Clarity Returning

Throat: Choice or Communication → Speaking Your Truth

Shoulders: Burdens about Self / Responsibilities → Thriving Returning

Arm Pits: I Can't / Lymphatic's → I Can and Do

Thyroid/Parathyroid: Anger → I Express My Anger

Thymus: Fear → I Have My Courage

Heart: Love Issues → I Give Love Freely

Liver, Gall Bladder: I Won't / Resentment → I Will Do This My Way

Spleen: It's Hard, I Can't / Self-esteem → This is Easy and I Can

Solar Plexus: Grief, Conscious Will → I Enjoy Doing This

Navel: Being Fed, Nourished → I Am Nourished

Solar Center: Deep Grief, Sub-conscious Will → I Will Myself To Do This

Gonads: Sexuality, Creativity, Procreativity, Essence, Self-Values → I Am the Creator

MALE/FEMALE SELVES

Each side of the body, meaning Left and Right halves, has different meanings related to our Un-conscious mind. Taking the time to understand each, gives deeper insight into what your Un-conscious mind is dealing with and what it is trying to tell you through signs or symptoms.

Right Side/Left Brain	Left Side/Right Brain
Ask, *IS it about…?*	
Giving	Receiving
Male	Female
Dad	Mom
Mundane	Creative
Rational	Intuitive
Linear	Imaginative
Active	Receptive
Out Going	In Coming
Feeding Others	Being Fed
Doing	Receiving
Inside the box	Outside the box
Exercising	Resting
Demanding	Nurturing
Closed	Open

Taking the time to learn these basics will go a long way toward deciphering what your body is communicating. As an example, a new practice member came to my office for her evaluation after driving with a friend for two hours to see me. She had agreed to come to the office because of the great progress her friend had made and how transformative her friend's results were. When she walked into the office, the first words out of her mouth, even before she met me were, *"This is the last time I am coming to this place!"* So I walked up and introduced myself and asked her why she said what she said. Her response was, *"It's too far and I don't have the time for this."* So I asked her what her health concern was. She stated, *"My right neck and shoulder have been painful for the past 20 years. I have had this problem and I have been to all sorts of different practitioners and had lots of counseling, and nothing is helping, so I figured if you could help my friend so much, perhaps you could help me."* Knowing what her body was communicating because of *Sacred Body Translations*, I asked her one question which immediately caused her to break into tears. My question was, *"How long have you been angry with your father?"* When she was able to regain her composure, she asked me, *"How would you know I have problems with my father?"* When I explained what her symptoms indicated, she was finally able to relax and focus on her issue, and then begin to let go of the Un-conscious belief system she had adopted that was causing her pain. When one is able to connect with some of the core issues people are dealing with, they will go to whatever lengths necessary to help themselves.

Next, we have more specifics related to different areas of the body and the Un-conscious mind. The Un-conscious mind will store emotions in many different areas and this next section also relates to some major areas of the body along with what each area means. Taking the time to learn these when paying attention to your own body will help you to understand what your Un-conscious mind is doing to get your attention for resolution. If you are helping others, these relationships will give you great insight into what the others are dealing with and the toll it is taking on them. If there is pain involved, this indicates they are not handling their issues. If asked, you can use some of the other tools covered to help facilitate their process of releasing their issues. Remember to always translate to your highest level of understanding. Most of all have fun with it.

Right and Left Body Language Basics

Right Temple	Left Temple
Right Choice about Giving and Doing (what to do)	Right Choice about Receiving

Right Ear	Left Ear
Hearing Linear, Rational, Male	Hearing, Nurturing, Creativity, Female

Right Shoulder	Left Shoulder
Burdens about Doing and Giving	Burdens about Receiving

Right Forearm	Left Forearm
Outgoing, Doing	Receiving, Doing

Right Wrist	Left Wrist
Flexibility in Handling, Doing	Flexibility in Receiving what's being given

Right Hand	Left Hand
Handling what is being Done or Given	Handling what is being Received

Right Thigh	Left Thigh
Understanding How to Move Forward To Do, Act or Give	Understanding How to Move Away from what you've Received

Right Knee	Left Knee
Forgive What's Happened or A Male Figure	Forgive What's Been Received or A Female Figure

Right Ankle	Left Ankle
Flexibility in stepping forward in life	Flexibility with stepping away from in life

Touching, feeling or having a symptom in any of these areas indicated can roughly be translated as indicated. For instance: Touching your right temple when having a thought is your Un-conscious mind contemplating making the right choice about what you are giving or doing. Pain, discomfort, swelling or perhaps breaking your left wrist would indicate a strong lack of flexibility with what life is giving you and asking you to handle. Pain, swelling or twisting your left ankle has to do with understanding and being flexible with stepping away from something in your life.

Self and Others

The front and back of the body represent where we store our imbalances related to ourselves or the stress related to our "perceived burdens" from others. Appreciate that the Un-conscious thoughts are held in the various areas of the body and are clues to what the "issue" will be, and if the issue is an issue of self or an issue related to how we perceive others. Notice the front of the body represents "self" from the head to the hips and "others" from the hips to the feet. Likewise, notice the back of the body represents "others" from the top of the head to the buttocks and "self" from the buttocks to the feet. Therefore, any tension, pain or restriction in the different areas either represents issues with self, or issues with how we perceive others. This is represented on the following page.

Others   I Can't

Self

Speaking/handling choices

Others   Responsibilities

Others   Resentment/I Won't

Self

Others   Kidneys: Forgiveness related to partnership

Self

Others   Letting Go/ Forgiveness/Support/ Emotional Holding/ Survival

Self

Others

Self

Others

Self

Others

Self

Others

Self

It would be important to notice where the tension is and then use the information given in this book to transform your body stress into positive outcomes. As an example, "perceived burdens" become "blessings returning." By reformatting your perception of the energy, you can take negative habit patterns stored within the body and transform them into something positive for you.

Head "*Sensibilities*"

When you are watching people or even when paying attention to yourself, you'll see that different aspects of our Un-conscious mind are always speaking through our body language. When we have an itch or feel a sensation in any of the areas of the face, we are indicating what our Un-conscious mind is feeling and then expressing. This is coming out of your Un-conscious mind, so therefore you are not fully conscious of it. If you pay attention, however, you can get a sense of what is going on in your or another person's Un-conscious mind. This helps you understand what is not being said, and how that may line up with what is being said.

Face and Head Language

When we take the time to notice what our head is doing in relationship to what is going on in our environment, we can again gain some insight into how we feel about what is happening. Take the time to observe the people in your life and gain some insights to what their Un-conscious mind is saying. When you have an opportunity, notice what is going on in yourself by looking in the mirror.

Head Slants Right:
Check to see if the 'doing/action' side of the body is being accentuated and the 'receiving/creative' side of the body is being moved away from.

Head Slants Left:
Check to see if the individual is pulling away from 'doing/action' side of the body, and is requiring or increasing creativity, nurturing or receiving.

Upper Forehead Contact:

Any contact with this part of the head, especially a full palm contact stimulates envisioning of something. Using the left hand is usually memory, while the right hand is related to creating or constructing.

The Cheeks:

These hold the ability to reveal our most immediate thoughts and feelings. Show what we feel. Think of being able to see someone "blush" when they are embarrassed.

Back of Head/Upper Neck Contact:

When contacted or stimulated by sensation, these frequently inducing memories of early survival patterns. Check birth memories, deep lack experiences growing up, trauma patterns from mom and dad. We call this Thriving Returning.

Jaw Hinge/TMJ:

Pain in the jaw joint or TMJ indicates conflict between feeling and thinking about what to do. This is the joining point of the conscious and sub-conscious expression.

Next we have body language related to our faces. Many times you have been able to tell how a person feels by looking at their face. A smile or a wrinkled brow is easy to interpret. When we see a person blush, we know that they are embarrassed. There are other clues as to what is going on within a person based upon the following parts of the face and what each corresponds to related to what is going on within the person's mind. Take the time to look at each aspect of the face, and spend some time learning to interpret for yourself what your face says about what you are dealing with in your Un-conscious mind. Any contact or sensation within each area corresponds to the meaning listed.

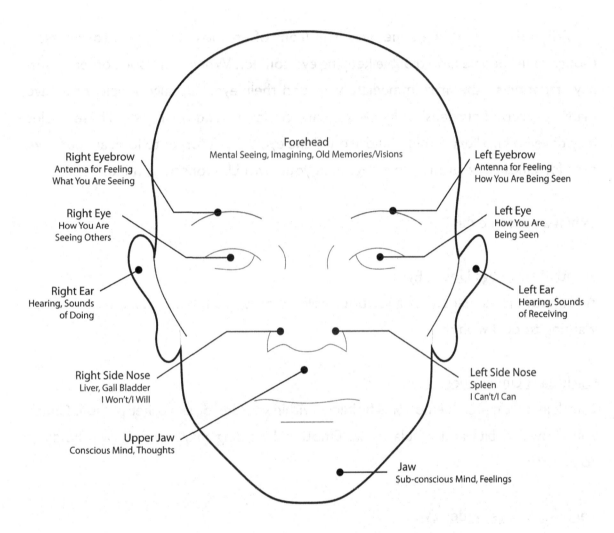

Forehead
Mental Seeing, Imagining, Old Memories/Visions

Right Eyebrow
Antenna for Feeling
What You Are Seeing

Left Eyebrow
Antenna for Feeling
How You Are Being Seen

Right Eye
How You Are
Seeing Others

Left Eye
How You Are
Being Seen

Right Ear
Hearing, Sounds
of Doing

Left Ear
Hearing, Sounds
of Receiving

Right Side Nose
Liver, Gall Bladder
I Won't/I Will

Left Side Nose
Spleen
I Can't/I Can

Upper Jaw
Conscious Mind, Thoughts

Jaw
Sub-conscious Mind, Feelings

Again, any contact with any of these areas either by yourself or the person you are observing is an indication of what is going on in the Un-conscious mind related to what the area of the face indicates. For example, if you rub your left eye when someone is speaking to you and you are using your left index finger, you are Un-consciously saying "*I am giving myself direction to see things in a new way.*" (see <u>Hands On</u> information for assistance with this translation pg. 87.)

When we look at someone who is in front of us, most are drawn to the eyes, though many people have trouble keeping eye contact. When you notice others' eyes, pay attention to the area immediately around their eyes. Usually people who have many "perceived burdens" will develop dark circles around their eyes. These circles may develop into "bags" under and around the eyes. Don't forget to look at your own eyes for clues to what may be going on in your own Un-conscious mind.

When a person exhibits:

<u>Slightly Dark Bags Under Eyes</u>:
Ask about emotional stress and about holding on to some emotional pain and not wanting to deal with it.

<u>Dark Bags Under Eyes</u>:
Check in on long-term emotional holdings within yourself or the other person. Check your bowel habits and regularity as Emotional holding may mean Bowel holding/ constipation.

<u>Very Dark Bags Under Eyes</u>:
These represent extreme emotional trauma for an extended period of time. If assisting others, find out how they spell "relief."

<u>Dark Eye Sockets</u>:
You or the individual may feel like giving up from the load of stress. You or they may feel like throwing in the towel about something. When you recognize this in someone

else, take the time to ask about what is going on in their life to help them release some of their burden.

The next aspect of the eyes to notice is how often they blink. Many times when talking with another, you will catch them blinking. This is normal, as blinking lubricates the eyes. When the blinking becomes repetitive, this indicates an issue. Most times, when you are touching on something that is very emotional for them, they will blink. The number of blinks will indicate the level of their communication. Pay close enough attention to their automatic blinking, and you will know what level of Un-conscious emotion they are expressing. Use your *Energy of Emotions* Chart to help understand the different levels being expressed.

Eye Blinks and Interpreting What They Mean

You will use this mostly when talking to other people. Pay attention with good eye contact.

Blinks:

1 Blink: Un-consciousness (usually 1 long blink)   **4 Blinks**: Fear

2 Blinks: Apathy (Low Self-Esteem)   **5 Blinks**: Anger

3 Blinks: Grief   **6 Blinks**: Pain

This is the reverse order of the *Energy of Emotions* Chart.

How To Use Material On Self:

As you begin to integrate the information you just read, the more your Consciousness will increase, the more aware you will become of what your Un-conscious body is telling you and what your Un-conscious body is asking you to assimilate. It is so much fun to recall and re-member (meaning to become a member again) within yourself. Have fun with it and be patient with yourself. Go to www.masterysystems.com for more information. This is the best information I know that is out there on the subject of Body Language and its interpretation.

Back Language

Our back is all about support from others (outside the body). The level of physical challenge reveals the level of suppression of our feelings and thoughts. As we become aware of how important feelings of being supported by others is to humanity, those who have participated in the study of Body Language Translations have come to a new understanding of the Divine role of being supported and supporting others. Body Language Translation is sacred. See perfection as you "translate" yourself and others.

The following are different areas of the brain and spine. The first two below represent areas of the brain and back of your skull. Your spine is then broken down into 4 main sections. These are from top to bottom, your Cervical spine or C-spine, which contains 7 vertebrae and are found within your neck; your Thoracic spine or your T-spine, which contain 12 vertebrae and are found where your ribs are; your Lumbar spine or your L-spine, which contain 5 vertebrae and is located in your low back; and finally your Sacral spine or S-spine which is at the base of your spine within your pelvis, between your hips.

Getting to know what each part of the spine is and how it correlates to how you relate to the world becomes important. Note the different relationships in the next two sections and see if you can find reasons for imbalances within your specific vertebrae

Pineal, Pituitary and Hypothalamus	Connection of Pain and Enthusiasm
Occiput	Heart, Love Issues
C1-C2	Medulla, Reptilian Brain, Survival Patterns
C 6	Burdens about "I Can't" Shoulder muscles, Tonsils
C 7	Thyroid, Parathyroid, Resisted Anger from Others
T 1	Speaking, Handling Choices
T 2	Love Issues, Flow of Love
T 3	Survival, Birth
T 4	Resentment, I Won't

T 5	Will, Energy, Life Force, Grief
T 6	Taking Things In, Assimilation
T 7	Grief, Joy, Sweetness
T 8	Apathy, I Can't, Conscious Will
T 9	Grief, Allergies, Stress
T 10	Forgiveness, Partnership
T 11	Letting Go, Forgiveness
T 12	Utilizing, Moving, Assimilating
L 1	Emotions, Holding/Letting Go
L 2	Enthusiastic Movement
L 3	Creativity/Procreativity
L 4	Support/Sexual Issues
L 5	Understanding, Moving Forward
Sciatic Nerve	Bowels and Emotional Holding

Next we have relationships within the spine that focus on how and where we hold onto emotional experiences; and what happens when they are suppressed into our Un-conscious minds. Each vertebrae represents something different. Unless you are a Chiropractor or other health care practitioner who is interested in translating the body, you probably have no reason to know what each vertebrae means specifically. However, when you do have a pain or discomfort in a specific vertebrae, this information can be helpful in determining what the underlying Un-conscious cause and its associated issue can be.

Spine Relationships

C1	Knowing, **Avoid doing what you know to do**
C2	Can't know, Can't imagine; Don't want to See, Hear, Speak/Be Seen or Heard
C3	Showing emotions to others, Sounds of others; Assimilation of what is known/felt
C4	Grief about knowing or not knowing; Resentment over what is said, heard, not felt
C5	**Speaking what you know**

C6	Doing what you know, and knowing what you are doing; Burdens, Apathy
C7	Anger from others, Anger toward others; Metabolism and energy to Know and Do
T1	Handling, Speaking
T2	Love Issues
T3	Survival, Birth; Mothering; Emotional Protection
T4	**Resentment**
T5	Energy, Resentment; Will; Grief; Life Force
T6	Taking things in; Assimilation; Holding without using
T7	Grief; Joy; Sweetness utilization
T8	Apathy; I Can't; Conscious Will
T9	Grief; Allergies; Stress
T10	**Forgiveness; Partnership**
T11	Letting Go; Forgiveness
T12	Utilization; Assimilation; Being Able to Move
L1	Holding on to Emotions; Emotionally Letting Go
L2	Enthusiastic Movement; Moving Forward
L3	Creativity; Pro-Creativity; Sexuality; Survival; Flexibility; Forgiveness
L4	Support Issues; Sexuality Issues; Creative Understanding; Emotional Holding
L5	**Flexibility in Understanding and Moving Forward**
Sacrum	Flexibility in Moving Forward; Sitting things out; Getting the Body Going
Coccyx	Letting Go with Ease

Taking time to become familiar with what each vertebrae means can be the key to unlocking some of our Un-conscious health issues. Study the relationships. They become important for you and the people you touch in your life. Once again, have fun with it.

Our hands are another aspect of our body which is always communicating. Many people use them to express how they are feeling. The hands are very expressive and different gestures can communicate a wealth of information. Giving someone the "*bird*" is an expression we all have seen and probably used at one point or another. When you begin to understand what the *Sacred Body Translation* for that specific finger is, you might laugh at what you have been communicating. Take the time to become familiar with what each finger represents, both for the left and the right hand, and begin considering these concepts. There is a wealth of information coming and going through our hands. Learning to interpret and translate what your hands and the hands of others are saying is important. Again, have fun and pay attention to what your hands are saying.

Resting Hand Positions

A resting hand having fingers that are tightly contracted in toward the palm usually has some issue about "holding on" to something. Check which hand and which fingers are most tightly closed. Resting hands that allow the fingers to be open and relaxed usually indicate ease with what the individual is handling in his or her life. Notice the variation between right and left hands. Remember the left hand is your "receiving" hand and your right hand is your "giving" hand.

Hands On

Pay Attention To Open and Closed Hands
As well as Fingers and Their Meanings

	Left Hand	Right Hand
	Receiving	**Giving**
Thumb:	Will to Receive	Will to Do and Give
Index:	Being Directed	Directing Others
Middle:	Receiving GOD given Strengths	Sharing GOD given Strengths
Ring:	Receiving Help form Others	Helping Others
Pinky:	Sex, Money, Desires	Sex, Money, Desires

First (tip) Phalange	Second (middle) Phalange	Third (base) Phalange
Mental Conception	Practical Execution /Action	Relating to Self Physically
Relates to Cortex	Practical Application	Relating it to Ourselves

Backs of Hands/Fingers: About Others

Palms of Hands/Fingers: About Self

Index Finger: **Left**: giving myself direction to receive from others/receiving directions from others. If I point at myself with my left index finger, let's say to my eye, I am directing myself to see things in a new way based on what others are saying to me.

Right: directing myself or others to Be, Do or Have, as when pointing in a direction.

Tapping Tips of Fingers: stimulating the Cortex of the brain for Mental Conception/ Thinking

Mounds (area) below fingers on the palm side: taking it all the way into yourself—embodying.

Closed Hands: represent shutting down and blocking communication; being defensive.

Play with this information and see what you and others are really saying using "hand language."

Shoulder Language

Finally, we finish up this section with understanding our shoulders. Since most people store their stress in their shoulders and upper backs with taking on the burdens of others, appreciating what the different sides mean and what it translates into is important. Pay attention when you are talking to others and what they do with their shoulders. And don't forget to notice for yourself what your shoulders are doing and where you keep all of your tension.

Right Shoulder Up: Are you worried about burdens of having to do something? Are you much more relaxed with feminine energy (left) and more uptight about masculine or work related situations (right)?

Both Shoulders Up: Are you holding onto burdens in most every area of your life right now? Do you perceive tension on all sides of you? Are or were your Mom and Dad at odds with each other in such a way as you have not felt supported by either of them?

Left Shoulder Up: Are you struggling with the responsibility of having to receive something? Do you feel stress with the burdens of a female figure? Do you have tension about allowing yourself to be creative and intuitive? Do you struggle with being able to receive what life offers?

Both Shoulders Down: Do you feel balanced with your responsibilities in life? Do you, or did you have a supportive relationship with both Mom and Dad? Do you feel up to the task of your life and ready to shoulder your responsibilities? Are you giving up on something within your life?

What Level Are You Coming From?

A piece of information mentioned earlier in the book was about the levels of self that are being expressed in what we say. Please review of what each word means when used in conversation; what it says about the level of consciousness being expressed and accessed.

ME: **Subconscious**
MYSELF: **Conscious**
I: **Higher self**

Pay attention to this yourself. Knowing what you are saying and knowing which level of self-talk you are communicating with is important to help re-solve all your Un-conscious emotional baggage that no longer serves you. Therefore, when you are using the word "me," you are speaking directly to and from your Un-conscious mind. The more you become aware of this within yourself, the more you can use the tools within this book to transform your Un-conscious ramblings into Conscious Language with improved outcomes.

Pearls Of Wisdom

Finally, I have a section coined by several of my practice members who have come to my FREE Health Care Classes to learn more about what their body is telling them. These are known as the *Pearls of Wisdom* and are things I have picked up over the years that came to me from specific sources I do not recall. Regardless of their source, they continue to prove out within my life and my practice. See if this is true for you as well.

Thyroid Issues: Suppressed anger—gave up your will/power—use the phrase, "*They won't let me!*" Statements involving "*They, He, She did this to me*" is **Thyroid Suppressed**

Calcifications within the body are associated with Thyroid/Parathyroid imbalances.

Ask yourself "*What authority are you reclaiming (authority expressed)?*" "*What new choice are you making about your own new authorship?*"

Coughing, as a symptom, is an indication you are accessing your Will and the energy is '*trying*' to be expressed. Ask yourself, "*What do I choose to say now?*" Then make sure you say it.

Sinuses: All congestion is associated with you *holding back* from being Inspired: you are stopping your Creative Genius from being expressed.

Mucus represents an "*I Can't*" mentality when out of balance. Dairy, cheese, milk, wheat, and pizza are foods that support the mentality of "*I Can't.*"

"*I Can't*" upgrades to → **I Can; or I am Clear**

Liver represents **"*I won't*"** mentally when out of balance and upgrades to → **I Will**

Spleen represents **"*I can't*"** mentally when out of balance and upgrades to → **I Can**
    I can't and *I won't* are a common way of thinking when confronted with life's opposition.

Yawning: This is our automatic waking up to what we are thinking and feeling. Being Inspired. The urge to yawn when others are speaking is cuing your Un-conscious to look at things a new way.

Re-Sent-Ment: represents something you have been given by life or someone which you would like to send back or re-send to the giver, but cannot.

Tensor Fascia Lata or TFL: A tendonous band on the lateral thigh, pain in this area of the body represents emotional holding.

RASH: anywhere on the body is an irritation about something you are feeling or didn't feel and have internalized, usually anger.

Grinding Teeth: represent parasitic thoughts. You are picking up doubt from other people. There is a Conflict between what you are thinking and what you are feeling. There is a "*pair of sites*" (sights) or two different perspectives. The other person's perspective is influencing how you see and act in your world.

Ankle(s) represent flexibility with stepping forward in life (right side) or away from something in life (left side). Relate this to UNDERSTANDING because your feet help you "*stand under*" yourself.

The phrase "*I get to…*" represents Stress that is based in FEAR. Pay attention to that when you use it yourself or hear it from others.

LOVE is the only MOTION; everything else is **E-Motion;** therefore, come from a state of love and your life will really begin to move in a positive direction.

Our Greatest weakness is our Greatest Strength yet to be discovered

Voice your Choice and speak your truth, always and all ways

Our body is our Keyboard of Consciousness. When we contact an area of the body, we are becoming aware of what is returning; i.e. rebooting. When we touch the body with our hands, palms and/or fingers, we are literally putting "*light*" into that part of our body. We are giving it healing energy. We are *Enlightening* that part of us. So when a part of the body hurts and we touch it, we are helping it return to harmony. The larger the symptom, the further out of balance and the more light it requires to restore harmony.

Symptoms are only present until we restore harmony within ourselves and restore ourselves back to our life course or stream.

So why do people develop health concerns and pains and dysfunction within their body? When you can appreciate what controls the way the body expresses itself (our thoughts and beliefs), being in harmony vs. being out of harmony begins to make sense. Any time you are not feeling well, you have gone out of agreement with yourself. Any time you have a pain or a symptom, you have gone out of agreement with yourself. Any time you have a disease, you have really gone out of agreement with yourself. What you experience in life, as we have learned, is a direct extension of what we believe to be possible or not possible. When life has shown us what is not possible and we begin to develop for ourselves beliefs of what "*that*" says, we develop and then adopt certain core beliefs to enable us to "*survive*" our life. And it is our Negative Core Beliefs that limit our reach, quell our spirit of adventure and deaden our sense of wonder.

Negative Core Beliefs

Within these broad belief patterns, however, are hundreds of different, personal variations and it is when you are identifying yours, that things start to become much clearer about many of the major issues in your life. (See examples that follow)

NOTE: A **core belief** is always an "*I*" statement as in "*I am unlovable;*" a belief such as "*Nobody loves me*" is called a **supporting belief**, and is a prediction or forecast about what others will do or have done to us. If it were not for the core belief, we may well have been able to accept love and be loved. The untrue core belief is what helped make other people's reactions occur (through *the Law of Attraction*). This gives the core belief the 'appearance' of being true, (a self fulfilling prophecy) even though it is a projection from our Un-conscious mind.

The book "*Growing Awareness*" by John Bligh Nutting contains a set of step by step worksheets that have been thoroughly "*road tested*" by over 2000 individual clients. These enable you to identify in private your own particular core beliefs. As you work through the pages you will develop a much greater awareness of your core beliefs and how you are triggered. You also become aware of the way your automatic protectors (your inner selves) react to triggers and, as a result, how they control your life and play havoc with your relationships. For more information on these negative core beliefs, go to www.core-beliefs-balance.com/growing_awareness_book.htm

The following are examples of potential Negative Core Beliefs we have all experienced in our lives. Even if we think they are not a concern for us now, it is important to look at them. Make sure to give yourself the opportunity to change any potential Un-conscious blocks. This is important for your life process. Read through the following examples and make a margin note of, or highlight the ones you have heard yourself say to yourself. Then later on in the book, you can use some of the tools to look at each negative core belief to transform every one into your new positive core belief system.

Not good enough (incompetent)

I am no good; I can't get it right; I can't make it work (klutz); I can't fix it; I am not good enough; I am unsuccessful; I'm not valuable; I am inferior; I am nothing; I am worthless; I am invisible; I am insignificant.

Not good enough (unlovable)

I am not lovable; I am unacceptable; I am plain and dull; I am not special; I don't matter; I am unworthy; I am not interesting enough.

Don't know, Wrong

I don't know; I get it wrong; I am always wrong; I can't understand; I'm not understood; I am in the wrong place; I am no good; I am a mistake.

In danger or Not safe

I'm not safe; I am afraid; I am uncertain; I am vulnerable; I am helpless.

Unwanted, Different

I don't belong; I am unwanted; I am alone; I am unwelcome; I don't fit in anywhere; I don't exist; I'm nothing; I should not be here at all; I'm not anybody; I am left out; I am unsuitable; I am uninteresting; I am unimportant; I don't matter.

Defective, Imperfect, Bad

It's my fault; I am guilty; I am bad; I am not whole; I am imperfect; I am unattractive; I am flawed; I am stupid; I am awkward; I am slow; I can't be me; I'm not true; I'm dirty; I am ugly; I am fat; I'm shameful; I am unclean; I am useless; I am crazy; I have a mental problem; I am out of control; I can't make myself clear; I am mistaken; I am unbalanced; I will fail; I am a failure; I don't deserve to be loved; I don't deserve to be cared for; I don't deserve anything; There's something wrong with me.

Powerless, One-below

I can't do it; I can't; I am a victim; I am weak; I am powerless; I am a failure; I am ineffective; I don't have any choice; I am less than; I am helpless; I finish last; I am always number two; I am always one-below; I can't stand up for myself; I am inferior; I am a loser; I am inadequate; I can't say 'no.'

Other

I am a klutz (awkward); I am a schmuk (unsophisticated).

Typical Negative Core Beliefs

Most negative core beliefs are connected in a broad way with a feeling of lost self worth or of not being "*good enough because .....*" but it is the words that follow this phrase which are the most powerful. They describe your core issue and those two or three words can set up a negative pattern that you will bond to and repeat throughout your life, unless you can balance them with a positive pattern.

A *Supporting Belief* is a similar prediction about what other people will or won't do to you. It is not a core belief but closely linked.

Examples of Negative Core Beliefs

1. Not good enough (I am not safe)

I'm unprotected

I am afraid

I am vulnerable

I am helpless

Supporting beliefs and predictions

Nobody will protect me

Linked Issues: Safety; Security; Peace; harmony; vulnerability; protection

2. Not good enough (I don't belong)

I am unwelcome

I don't fit in anywhere

I am lost

I am all alone

I can't help myself

I am unwanted

I should not be here at all

Supporting beliefs and predictions

Nobody wants to know about me

Linked Issues: Belonging; Connection; Self- nurturing

Unbalanced core beliefs - general patterns

Unbalanced or negative beliefs can be very different from person to person. Some are quite unique. Most core beliefs however are connected in a broad way with a sense of having lost your self-worth or not being good enough:

Negative Beliefs or Feelings about myself/Bottom line issues

1. Not good enough (I am not safe)	Security; Safety
2. Not good enough (I don't belong)	Belonging, Nurture; Self care
3. Not good enough (I have no value, I am worthless)	Self worth
4. Not good enough (I am powerless)	Success; Power; Control
5. Not good enough (I am wrong, I am unsure)	Reality; Reason Knowing
6. Not good enough (My life is out of balance)	Balance; Moderation
7. Not good enough (I am defective)	Self worth and Deservedness
8. Not good enough (I don't exist; I am nothing)	Identity; Recognition
9. Not good enough (I am not real)	Self awareness
10. Not good enough (I am unlovable; unwanted)	Love, Loved and Loving
11. Not good enough (I am broken)	Health; Self-healing
12. Not good enough (I am not whole; I have lost my spirit)	Wholeness; Spirit

3. **Not good enough (I am worthless)**

I am disposable

I am unworthy

I am not worth anything

I am not interesting enough

I am no good

I'm nothing

I never come first

I'm not anybody

I am unimportant

I am uninteresting

I'm not valuable

I always come second

Supporting beliefs and predictions
Nobody values me
Nobody cares about me
People who say nice things to me don't
mean them

Linked issues: Self worth; Loyalty,
Difficulty giving or receiving gifts,
congratulations, love or appreciation;

4. **Not good enough (I am powerless)**

I am incompetent

I am not any good

I am unsuccessful

I am unworthy

I can't control anything

I am inferior

I am disposable

Supporting beliefs and predictions
There is no way out for me;
I can't achieve I will fail;
I can't change;
Other people manipulate me and
escape

Linked issues: Achievement; Boundaries;
Standards; Structure; Success; Goals, Re
control my life; I am trapped and cannot
sults; Being organized, Self empowerment;
self- protection; ability to make changes;
bonding patterns; avoiding manipulation;

5. **Not good enough (I am wrong, I am unsure)**

I don't know

I always get it wrong

I am always wrong

I am confused

I can't understand

I'm not understood

I am in the wrong place

I am a mistake

I am unaware

I am uncertain

I can't make myself clear

I am mistaken

I am not trustworthy

I can't be sure

Supporting beliefs and predictions

It isn't fair

I won't get justice

I can't trust people

People don't trust me

6. **Not good enough (My life is out of balance)**

I am unbalanced

I am out of control

I can't be moderate

I always get it wrong

Nothing works for me

I stuff up everything I do

I am a klutz

I can't fix it

Everything I do goes wrong I attract trouble

I have ruined my whole life

I can't get it right

I am in the wrong place

I can't make it work (klutz)

I can't fix it

I will never be able to fix it up

Supporting beliefs and predictions

Other people have to fix my life for me

Wherever I am I don't like it.

I need to move

Linked Issues: Truth; Right-wrong; Justice;

Fairness; Openness and honesty;

Trust and Trustworthiness; Integrity;

Understanding

Unbalanced core beliefs - general patterns

Unbalanced or negative beliefs can be very different from person to person. Some are quite unique. Most core beliefs however are connected in a broad way with a sense of having lost your self-worth or not being good enough:

NegativeBeliefsorFeelingsaboutmyself/Bottom line issues

1. Not good enough (I am not safe)	Security; Safety
2. Not good enough (I don't belong)	Belonging, Nurture; Self care
3. Not good enough (I have no value, I am worthless)	Self worth
4. Not good enough (I am powerless)	Success; Power; Control
5. Not good enough (I am wrong, I am unsure)	Reality; Reason Knowing
6. Not good enough (My life is out of balance)	Balance; Moderation
7. Not good enough (I am defective)	Self worth and Deservedness
8. Not good enough (I don't exist; I am nothing)	Identity; Recognition
9. Not good enough (I am not real)	Self awareness
10. Not good enough (I am unlovable; unwanted)	Love, Loved and Loving
11. Not good enough (I am broken)	Health; Self-healing
12. Not good enough (I am not whole; I have lost my spirit)	Wholeness; Spirit

Linked Issues: Fixing problems;
Solutions; Achievement;

7. **Not good enough (I am defective)**

It's my fault

I am bad

I am imperfect

I am flawed

I am awkward

I can't be me

I'm not true

I am ugly

I'm shameful

I am useless

I am crazy

I will fail

I am a loser

I don't deserve to be loved

I don't deserve anything

I am guilty

I am not whole

I am unattractive

I am stupid

I am slow

I am hopeless

I'm dirty

I am fat

I am unclean

I am a reject

I am unbalanced

I am a failure

I will lose Integrity; Reason;

I don't deserve to be cared for

Supporting beliefs and predictions
There's something wrong with me
People can tell there is something
wrong with me

Linked Issues:
Balancing giving and receiving;
Emotional age; Growth; Avoiding "flips"
between opposite positions; Understanding

8. **Not good enough (I don't exist, I am nothing)**

I am nothing

I am worthless

I am invisible

I don't exist

I'm nothing

I'm not anybody

I am insignificant

I am not enough

I am not recognized

Supporting beliefs and predictions
People cannot see me

Linked Issues: Recognition; Being who I really am; My history; My knowledge; My experience; Self-awareness; My doings are not my beings (Who I am is not what I do)

9. **Not good enough (I am not real)**

I am a fake

I don't know what is real

I am unsuitable

I don't know who I really am

I am not true

Supporting beliefs and predictions
People will find out that I am a fake

Linked Issues: Freedom; Autonomy; Individuality; Intimacy; Self-protection; Balancing my personal and impersonal energies

10. **Not good enough (I am unlovable; unwanted)**

I am not lovable

I am unacceptable

I am always left out

I don't matter

I am not special

I am not wanted

I don't matter

I am alone

I am unwelcome

I don't fit in anywhere

I am unsuitable

I am uninteresting

I am unimportant

I am plain and dull

Supporting beliefs and predictions
Nobody loves me
Nobody wants me

Linked Issues: Caring; Sharing; Unconditional loving; Balancing my giving and receiving;

11. **Not good enough (I am broken)**

I am no good

I am bad

I am crazy

I have a mental problem

I am going to die early in life

I am damaged (goods)

I am broken

I am unfixable, unrepairable

I cannot be healed

I am doomed

I am mentally defective

I am emotionally crippled

I am emotionally defective

Supporting beliefs and predictions

I am hurting, in pain

People can see that I am defective

Someone else will heal, fix or repair me

Unless you heal me I will never get better

Nobody can heal my pain

Linked Issues: Self healing, defects; perfection, pain

12. **Not good enough (I am not whole; I have lost my spirit)**

I am not whole

I have no integrity

I have no hope

I feel hopeless

I have lost my spirit

I can't grow

Nothing good ever happens to me

I am a bad person

I am sinful

I am evil

Supporting beliefs and predictions

There is nothing to hope for

I must not get my hopes up

Linked Issues: Integrity; Balance Wholeness; Spirit; Self- actualization; Spirit and spirituality; Personal Growth

Take the time to go through these one at a time and see which ones create a feeling within you. Typically, each one of these will apply to most people with some being more readily apparent than others. It would be in your best interest to look at each example and do some writing related to how each heading makes you feel and if there is any truth to the Negative Core Beliefs. Have fun with it, see what you discover and most of all, have compassion for yourself as you begin to reclaim your true identity and begin to watch your relationships and life change for the better.

These next two pages are designed to help you find your negative core beliefs. Make several copies of them and use them often. This is really where you are going to identify for yourself why your life is limited. This will help you to discover your Un-conscious programming that was given to you by your parents, teachers, siblings, friends and other people who have helped to shape your belief system. And remember, most, if not all of your beliefs were established before you were 7 years old. Therefore take the time to recall as much as you can from your childhood. Sometimes you will have to deal with recent, more active memories before you will have access to your childhood memories. Please appreciate that the process you will be going through is not simple. Spend the time to get in touch with your Un-conscious mind by accessing your Un-conscious memories. Finally, it is important for you to appreciate that no one ever does anything wrong, based on their model of the world. In other words, as we all look through our Un-conscious belief systems and see the world through a distorted perspective, we will all take action based upon what we believe is true. Therefore, having compassion for yourself for any *"mistakes"* you have made and likewise having compassion for what others have done is important to remember. Also - remembering that your life is 100 % about you and what you are putting out energetically allows you to let the others off the hook and allows you to take responsibility for your own creations.

Exercise # 4
Finding Your Negative Core Beliefs

Personal Activity Sheet Date:__/__/__ **Keep this sheet private. Show it only to supportive people**

What Is A Trigger? (Please read this first)

2. Then I Imagined:

A trigger is anything that regularly ignites immediate and strong reactions inside you for example: yelling, fighting, hitting, screaming, panic, running, hiding, total surrender, freezing or anything often brings on similar feelings such as extreme anger, rage, confusion, terror, worthlessness, devastation, emotional pain or extreme discomfort.

In this column, write what you then imagined about YOU or what you told yourself about YOU. For example   I imagined __ that I might get hurt again I knew I wasn't Important; I told myself it was all my fault; that I didn't matter.

1. When I Am Triggered...

What kind of comments by others, what specific events or actions, what situations, sounds or tone of voice, what kind of touch, or emotion, what kind of music or even a smell can trigger a reaction like these in you?
Below, describe some of these specific events (example: When Kim blamed me for losing the money.) Avoid general or vague examples such as: When I am blamed for losing things. Include events from throughout your life starting with recent ones and moving backwards in time.
Suggestions: When__said__to me; When __criticized me; When I had to do ___ to stop ___ getting angry; When ___ ignored me; When I was left alone by ___; When ___(who I love) is in pain; When no one even noticed me____; When ___ complimented me about__; When ___ yelled at me and lectured me about__; When I had to ___ in front of everyone; When ___ told me and I didn't understand; When I hear ___ playing on the radio; When I smell the aroma of ___; When ___ was so unfair about;

These are just some of the thoughts that can '*Hot wire*' straight into your most common reactions.

1. WHEN   >

2. WHEN   >

3. WHEN   >

4. WHEN   >

5. WHEN (for this one perhaps go back a few years)   >

6. WHEN I (for this one perhaps go back a few relationships)   >

7. WHEN I (for this one perhaps go back to your teen years)   >

8. WHEN I (for this one go back to your earliest memories)   >

Finding Your Negative Core Beliefs

3. Then I felt...

In this column, write what you then felt:

Examples: Hurt, Sad Pain, Panic, Fear, Alone, Guilt, Shame, Embarrassed, Confused, Frustrated, Angry, Terrified, Devastated, Annoyed, Worthless (These are just some of the feelings that switch on your reactions)

4. This is how I reacted or responded (my reaction patterns)

After you are triggered, what do you do automatically (instantly)? Noticing and naming your triggers and then your repetitive patterns are two of the best clues that in turn help you discover your own negative core beliefs. **Examples**: I got angry and yelled at... I became very quiet and didn't say a word. I started to cry. I said things to ___ that I knew would make them go away. I panicked. I told___ what I thought he/she wanted to hear. I got very calm and logical and tried to explain. I tried to control him/her. I criticized (attacked) ____ about his/her faults. I smiled and made a joke about it. I felt cold and started to shake. I hit him. I lied. I got drunk. I tried to think positive thoughts. I 'got even.' I sabotaged everything.

If you like, you can play with these four columns at random or in any order. You might start with this one (column 4) and move back to col. I or begin with col. 3

1.

2.

3.

4.

5.

6.

7.

8.

Now that you have taken the time to identify some of your negative core beliefs, it is important to do something to transform them into a positive; something you can be in agreement with; something you can be happy about; something that makes your heart sing and your life go forward the way you would choose for it to go forward. In order to make your heart sing, it is important to get out of your head and move into your heart. Once you know how to access your Heart Center, speaking from your heart allows you to be in alignment with your higher self/source self/GOD self. Once in alignment with your source energy, you will begin to manifest your hearts desires. Isn't that the true reason for taking the time to move through this material?

Toolbox Item # 6
Listening To Your Internal Guidance System

3   Different Ways of Listening to Yourself:

1. *Emotional Body* – this is automatic, and done without thinking. The quickest way to understand this aspect of listening to yourself is to pay attention to your automatic reactions, first thoughts or first words. This is purely instinctive and emotional without conscious control of your reactions. This is our Un-conscious mind.

2. *Thinking Mind* – using thought (typical way). This is slower and more deliberate, since each of us takes the time to compare what is happening to what we have previously experienced. We compare the two before we re-act. We are given the opportunity to think about our response OR we can simply re-act, as in knowing it is wrong and doing it anyway.

3. *Eternal Self* – here you will find your connection to your *Internal Guidance System. It requires you to get really present and feel your answers rise to the surface of your consciousness.* This type of response is typically very slow in coming and has a different quality then the first two. When you "*experiment*" with this way of responding, you will begin speaking from your heart more and more. People will feel the sincerity of your words and will respond in alignment with your intention.

You did some of this at the beginning of this book. I asked you to take the time to discover "*Why are you really here?*" If you still haven't taken the time to access that part of you, your Core Self, your Heart Center and your connection to Source Energy, please do so now. I cannot emphasize enough how your life will begin to change once you take the time to learn where your Heart Center is; and how to come from your heart, without ego or a hidden agenda. These are the tools of the mind. Once you are fully in your heart, you will never again use the ego for self gain. Once in the heart, your ego drops away and falls in line with what is your highest and best, and aligns with everyone else's highest and best.

By combining Toolbox Item # 4 **Decreeing** with Toolbox Item # 6 **Your Internal Guidance System**, you will begin to feel your way into your desired outcome. We have seen that feelings are what allow each of us to create our outcomes achieved. Focusing on your feelings consciously and then expressing them verbally will begin to replace old 'negative' habit patterns of thinking with new 'positive' habit patterns of creating. Continued positive thinking will begin to transform your outcomes experienced.

Next we have our Toolbox item which is called *The Freedom Process*. This tool is used to open yourself up to possibilities. When you are in a negative place, you have the tendency to limit yourself and think in terms of what is not possible. This will hinder your progress in life. It will also influence what you experience in an extremely negative way by shutting you down and closing you off to your source/creative energy. When you feel this has happened, use *The Freedom Process* to help you move forward with effective, encouraging questions. When done consciously, you will gain access to new and expansive possibilities which, when acted on, will create new and desired outcomes. Play with this tool for yourself, and you will also find it quite useful when helping to facilitate others.

Toolbox Item # 7
Helpful Outcome Focused Questions/ The Freedom Process

Note: When you are caught up in a negative thought form (or story or belief that is not serving you), you will often use *Limiting Language* to express your feelings. Sometimes it is helpful to ask questions that encourage you to come up with your own Outcome-Focused (Creative Choice) answers. Your answers can open up new declaratives to use with Decreeing.

The following example questions are very helpful to get you into your feeling of having your outcome already:

- If you say, "*I can't, I never get it right, etc.,*" then ask yourself: "*What if I could?*" "*What would happen if I did?*"
- *Now that I am having, doing or being _____ (fill in the outcome), what is new and different in my life? What am I feeling as a result?*
- If you want to change your negative feeling or situation ask, "*What is my outcome of having, feeling, doing or being _____?*" Keep asking the same question to every answer until you have discovered your true outcome.

Once you have read through some of the Outcome Focusing questions to open you up to possibilities, take the time to do Exercise # 5. The Freedom Process is exactly what it says; it gives you freedom to *have, do, be* and *feel* whatever you desire from your heart and to begin manifesting those outcomes that are important to you.

Exercise # 5
The Freedom Process

Helpful Outcome Focused Questions

Is there anything that is keeping me from being fully and completely present, Yes or No? When No, state "*I am fully and completely present.*"

If YES, go through the following exercise:

My withhold is I feel _____ (emotion involved) about_____ because _____ (reason(s) - answer the because 3X's to 3 levels of understanding) and my choice NOW is to transmute THE _____ (original emotion) into MY _____ (counterpart of the emotion) and I empower (myself or others) to _____ with _____ (qualities, feelings which sustain the positive).

For example:

My withhold is I feel <u>angry</u> about <u>my life situation</u> because <u>I can't move my life forward</u> because <u>I don't have the money to buy the new equipment</u>, because <u>my business is down</u>, because <u>I am not focused enough to generate new business</u>, and my choice NOW is to transmute THE <u>anger by forgiving myself</u> for not focusing on getting new business, and <u>I take MY authority</u> to put my distractions aside and I empower myself to <u>take action to generate new business</u> with <u>conscious loving action from now on</u>.

Some Emotions and Their Upgrades

Enthusiasm: full of pure joy and love (your outcome emotion after upgrading)

1) Pain → upgrades through feeling the pain (Breathe it, Feel it, Love it) → **Love, Intuition**

2) Anger, Resentment, Frustration, Irritation, and **Aggression** (they did this to me....) →upgrades through **FORGIVENESS** → **Authority, Loving Action**

3) Fear, Dread, Terror, Paralyzed Will, Impending Doom (What if...) →upgrades through feeling (Breathe it, Feel it, Love it) → **Courage, Trust, Faith, Security**

4) Grief, Sadness, Yearning, Anguish, Sorrow → upgrades through feeling (Breathe it, Feel it, Love it) → **Joy, Happiness**

5) Apathy, Depression (I can't, it's too hard) → upgrades through feeling (Breathe it, Feel it, Love it) → **Ease, Caring**

6) Un-conscious (I don't know, I'm numb) → upgrades through feeling (Breathe it, Feel it, Love it) →**Consciousness**

See Your *Energy of Emotions Chart* for more examples (pg. **31**)

The next tool is really powerful. It helps you to use your mind to focus your heart into knowing what your true desires are and the reasoning behind them. It helps you move through several different layers and arrive at the real reason for desiring anything in your life. It is called Outcome/Mind Mapping, and helps to get you into your outcome.

Toolbox Item # 8
Outcome/Mind Mapping

Use the following Tool for Yourself to find out What Your True Outcome Is

Mind mapping is a tool to help us use the right and left halves of our brain simultaneously. This should be done using a big blank piece of white paper or poster board with several different colored markers and in a quiet room with no distractions.

This is **YOUR Process**.

- Place your heart's # 1 top priority in the center of the paper
- Use images 2 represent words when applicable (symbols R powerful)
- Use curvy lines coming out of the center 2 represent each different outcome, meaning *"What is New and Different?"*
- Use a different color for **each branch coming off the center**
- Use no more
  than 3 words
    per line
      PRINTING clearly
- With Every Line, ask yourself, "What is my outcome for having this?" Then write it down and ask yourself the question again and again from having that outcome achieved. ("What is my outcome of having my outcome?"). Keep asking the same question through many layers until you get to what is really important. Repeat this for every line on your mind map.
- Go ahead and break the "rules" once in a while if it helps you achieve clarity. If you feel resistance to filling in a line, this is a great spot to RELEASE the resistance. Refer to Toolbox Item # 3 **Releasing** (pg. 61)

NOW MY PASSION IS FLOWING FREELY, WHAT AM I BEING, DOING, HAVING AND FEELING; WHAT IS NEW AND DIFFERENT?

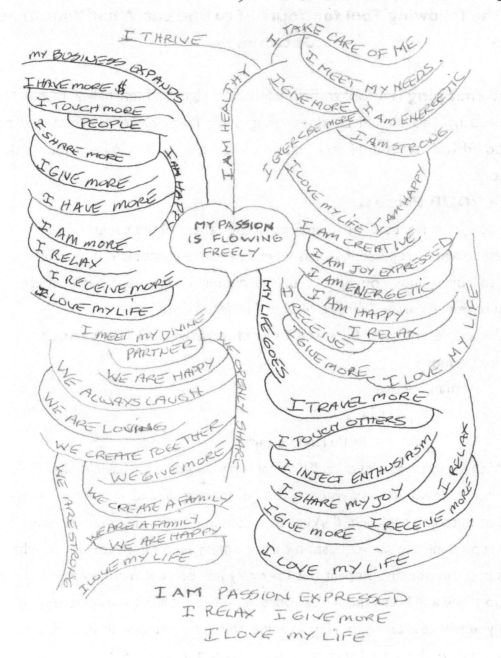

I AM PASSION EXPRESSED
I RELAX I GIVE MORE
I LOVE MY LIFE

Exercise # 6
Outcome/Mind Mapping

Use the following Exercise for Yourself to find out What Your True Outcome Is

Mind Mapping or Outcome Mapping is an exercise to help us use the right and left halves of our brain simultaneously. This allows us to be both creative and intuitive as we think. This is one possible use for mind mapping. There are many more, and I encourage you to explore others.

Using a blank sheet of paper or poster board, do the following exercise for every different aspect of your life you would choose to improve. Begin by placing your heart's number one top priority for your life in the center of the page. Draw a shape around your outcome, which represents your desire; for example, if your outcome involves money, then a dollar sign could be a good symbol. Increased lung capacity could be represented with a blown up balloon. A new loving partner could be represented with a heart. Inside your symbol write what your desired outcome is. This should be brief and to the point (a couple of words or a short phrase that captures the essence of your desired outcome)

From the symbol of your outcome, draw lines, which represent your desired effects of HAVING your outcome achieved. Each major branch should be drawn in a different color. Each line is best done with 3 words per line to make it easier for your mind to process. If you have more than 3 words, have it branch off of the original to finish the sentence (See Example). Go ahead and break the "rules" once in a while if it helps you achieve clarity. This is **YOUR Process**.

- Place your heart's # 1 top priority in the center
- Use images 2 represent words when applicable (symbols R powerful)
- Use curvy lines coming out of the center 2 represent each different outcome, meaning "What is New and Different?"
- Use a different color for **each branch coming off the center**
- Use no more
  than 3 words
    per line
      PRINTING clearly

- With Every Line, ask yourself, *"What is my outcome for having this?"* Then write it down and ask yourself the question again and again from having your outcome achieved. (*"What is my outcome of having my outcome?"*). Keep asking the same question through many layers until you get to what is really important. Repeat this for every line on your mind map.
- Go ahead and break the "rules" once in a while if it helps you achieve clarity. If you feel resistance to filling in a line, this is a great spot to RELEASE the resistance. Toolbox Item # 3 **Releasing** (pg. 61)

I cannot over emphasize the power of this exercise. By taking the time to activate both halves of your brain, you really begin to balance it and come into sync with what is your heart's desire. By balancing both the feminine and masculine aspects; the creative and the linear; the intuitive and the logical; you will begin to create the type of outcomes you've always dreamed of having. Remember that things can change pretty quickly. Also keep in mind that sometimes things need to fall away before the new desired outcomes can take their appropriate place in your life. Enjoy your creative process, your self-discovery and your outcomes achieved.

Now, we move onto our next important tool. This tool is something we all have used at various times in our lives, and for most, it hasn't been used properly since early childhood. All of us have pretended and created imaginary scenarios in our lives. It is through our imagination that new ideas and possibilities are born. All of our *"reality"* observed was once an idea born in imagination. Furthermore, the more you *"play"* with your imagination, the more your creative possibilities can begin to manifest. Once the ball starts moving, the momentum that results is transformative.

Consider the following tool when choosing to create something new and exciting in your life.

Toolbox Item # 9
Using Imagination To Create Your Life

Be SPECIFIC in your imagination of your desires.

Remember to seek first your heart's true desire and imagine from there.

Imagine yourself *doing, being* or *having*, while *feeling* your desires fulfilled.

Gregg Braden says it takes **thoughts, feelings and emotions** to manifest and attract what it is you desire. All of these things are focused through imagining from your wish fulfilled.

Having read the information, I'm sure your mind is already beginning to create. Take time to capitalize on your creative energy and do the next exercise, Exercise # 7 right now for your heart's number one top priority. Perhaps you can do this with some of your other desires and you can do it on the heels of your previous exercise, Exercise # 6 Outcome/Mind Mapping, now that you know what your true desires are. By using your imagination in this way, you begin to build on the creative energy and more possibilities with creative consciousness come into your awareness.

My Dream Car

When I was 5 years old, I saw a car while my parents were driving us to a family event. The car I saw was a Porsche 911 and it looked different than all the other cars I had ever seen. Somewhat like a Volkswagon Beetle, except it looked faster and more exciting. In the moment I saw it, I decided I really liked it and one day I would have one. As time went on and I got older, I never lost sight of that desire to have one of those cars. And as time went on, the design of the car became more sporty and being a car enthusiast, I would look for it in the various car magazines my father would buy. And what seemed like every year I would see at least one of these Porsche 911 sports cars and the subtle changes from year to year made me desire it more. When I got my driver's license, I would always image what it would be like to drive a Porsche 911 and by now I wanted a Turbo. When I went away to college, I continued to desire the car and when I was home for break, I would go to a Porsche Dealership and talk with one of the sales people I became friends with. He would let me sit in any of the Porsches I wanted and would always give me brochures of the newest Porsche 911 Turbo to take with me when I went back to school. When I got to Grad School, I took the pictures of the newest Porsches and placed them in frames and then hung them on my walls of my apartment. I would always look at them and imagine what it would feel like to drive one of the turbos on a windy road. I could feel the rev of the engine under my right foot, the comfort of the seat wrapped around me and the exhilaration of the experience of driving this incredible car and speeding through the corners. I was going to have one of these cars.

When I graduated Chiropractic School and went into practice, I would still go to the dealership and talk with my friend and we would discuss the cost of such a venture. I wasn't ready to purchase because I had other priorities, and I continued to appreciate the concept of owning a Porsche 911 Turbo.

One day, my dad called me and asked me if I was to buy a Porsche, what model would I get? I said that was easy, the Porsche 911. He asked me what color would I get? I said either Charcoal Grey or Black with a black interior. He then said, what else would I get related to it? I said it would be a turbo and it would have a fin on the back. Then I asked him why? He said, "When you come down to the house, you'll see one in the garage," as he had just leased one. Needless to say, I drove down to his house to see what was my dream car sitting in his garage. When he showed it to me, as we talked about it, he asked me if I would like to take it for a drive. I was thinking he would drive it and let me sit in the passenger seat. Then he handed me the keys and said, "Let's go for a drive." I couldn't believe it. I was about to drive my dream car. We went for a drive and I even got to scare him a little as I accelerated onto the highway to feel what this powerful beast felt like. When we got back to the house, I said, "That is an awesome car." He asked if I ever thought I could own something like that, and I said, "Right now I don't think I could be responsible enough, as I like speed too much." This was my Limited Belief System kicking in. And over the next couple of years, I thought about it a lot. I imagined what I would have to "be" in order to own that car. I imagined what I would have to "do" in order to own that car. And I imagined what I would have to "have" in order to own that car. I then began thinking a lot about it and began saving for it. I actively put away every dollar I could when I could to save for owning that car. This was funny, because about a month or so later, my dad took me and my older brother to Road Atlanta Raceway to the Porsche Driving School where we spent a day doing various exercises driving the Porsche 911. Probably one of the best days of my life, and certainly the most fun. Where else can you go to drive as hard and as fast and an exotic sports car and not have to worry about anything happening? Having the opportunity to drive a Porsche on a racetrack and to race at speeds faster than allowed on the highways…this was heaven. When we were at the airport headed home, my dad shared with me that if I felt ready when his lease was up, he had already negotiated the buyout price for the Porsche 911 Turbo he was leasing. Again, I didn't know if I was responsible enough to own a car like that, and that was the real reason for me changing my intention. Knowing what I had to come up with money wise, I now had a goal in mind. I knew the money required and I knew the timeframe in which I needed to have it in. And when the day came that it was time to purchase the Porsche 911 Turbo, I did. Paying for it outright was a great feeling. Getting behind the wheel and driving it home was like floating on air. It seemed like a dream. It was a dream…it was My Dream Car. I was the owner and it belonged to me. And now I race the car with various car clubs at several different tracks a year. All the focusing, wishing and dreaming had come true. What began in my imagination as a little 5 year old had finally manifested before my 40th birthday. Dreams do come true if you allow them to. Put your intention into an idea and don't worry about the "how" and your dreams can come true. The *Law of Attraction* says so.

Exercise # 7
Using Imagination To Create Your Life

Teach Yourself How To Imagine From Your Outcome Fulfilled Using The Following Exercise

Neville, an early 1900's author, says if you "imagine from your wish fulfilled," you will create (or attract) what you desire faster. The movie, *The Secret*, talks about this as well. In the following exercise you will use this tool in a written example (use a separate sheet of paper for more room). By activating your imagination, you are accessing your creative consciousness and putting it in sync with your heart's desires.

Take a moment to pause, take a deep breath, clear your mind, drop into your heart and begin -

Imagine you were conceived during an act of perfect love between your parents. Imagine your parents planned for you and were happy you came into their lives to bless them. Imagine your entire family was there at your birth, welcoming you into the world. Imagine you were treated with respect as you grew up. Imagine you were given full authority of your life by the time you were 16 years old.

Take a moment to feel your imagination working. You may feel different sensations in your body. Remember, feeling is key to attracting what you desire. Using your imagination is a great way to create feeling.

Now, imagine 5 years ago a genie or an angel granted you your outcome that you wished for at the beginning of this book. Imagine you have had it with you or within you in every moment over the past 5 years. You have had and lived your wish. Describe what you are *doing, being, feeling* and *having* now that you have lived this way for 5 years.

Write down **WITH SPECIFICS** where you are, what you are *doing, having, being* and most important, what you are *feeling* in your newly imagined state.

_____

_____

_____

_____

_____

_____

_____

_____

_____

_____

_____

_____

_____

_____

_____

_____

Having done this exercise, we have now opened ourselves up to imagining things that will make our future brighter and allow us to feel inspired going forward. This is important, for life is always pulling you forward and leading you to your highest self expressed. I hope this is becoming clear for you.

Another interesting and powerful concept to consider is "*Rewriting Your History.*" This is a powerful tool and one that has made a huge difference for me in my life. Sometimes we have had a traumatic event occur in our lives which has caused us to limit our ability to reach for the numerous intentions we have gone into agreement with. This makes the cycle of repetition seem impossible to overcome. Taking the time to Re-write Your History is an authoritative way to take back your power and lose the victim mentality, thus allowing you to forgive anyone who "may have been the cause of" your life circumstance.

Toolbox Item # 10
Re-writing Your History

Remember, what you BELIEVE about your history up to now is what will create your focus for NOW. Your NOW FOCUS dictates your FUTURE experience.

One effective way to get you into a "*new view*" of your life is to revise your memory of your history. STOP telling your same "*old story*" and simply and calmly write a "*New One.*"

The more "*real*" you can imagine it, the more it will change your Un-conscious beliefs. As we have seen, by changing your Un-conscious beliefs, you will change your NOW focus and your Future experience of you.

Having your authority in your life means to take "*authorship*" over your experience. Notice the root word "*author*".

As author of your life, you write your life which you choose to have.

The following is a personal example I used in my life when re-writing my history. Appreciate the example of *My Vanishing Twin* I used is more common in society than many would think. I invite you to do a key word search for "Vanishing Twin" on the internet and do some reading. Perhaps you too could be one. Either way, developing the highest form of love, which is compassion for yourself and another, will allow you to let go of your attachment to people showing up for you in a particular way and allow you to take back your power. It allows you to become your highest authority as you begin to author your life going forward.

My Vanishing Twin

When I was in utero with my twin, we had chosen to come into this world together with the agreement we would go forth into our new life to create an awesome life together. In the process of our first 3 months my twin received a message from OUR FATHER, asking him to "come home." My twin felt conflicted with his situation. After all, he had made an agreement with me to go into our life together, and now OUR FATHER was calling him home. He took the attitude of choosing to stay and play with me some more, and we had fun discussing why OUR FATHER wanted him home this early. He thought that perhaps he had upset OUR FATHER and perhaps he was in trouble. I reassured him OUR FATHER loves each of us unconditionally and he had nothing to worry about because of OUR FATHER's unconditional love. Then he said, "*But what about our agreement? I said I would do this with you, and now OUR FATHER is calling me home. I don't want to go home; I want to stay with you.*" I reassured him again that we could always co-create together and that OUR FATHER, "*If he is calling you home, knows there is always plenty of time to co-create with me, and whatever the reason for calling you home, it must be both exciting and important.*" He still wasn't convinced he could leave me. So we talked some more and I asked him, "*Do you trust OUR FATHER?*" He said, "*YES!*" I said, "*Do you trust OUR FATHER to know what is BEST for both you and myself?*" He said, "*YES!*" "*And because that is true, and because he has called you home and not me, there must be a great reason for you to go home, and for me to go forth without you into my next life; To go forth without you by my side.*" My twin felt a little better, and still had some apprehension about me going forth without him. I reassured him I would be O.K. and I would do it for both him and myself. And I asked him to honor OUR FATHER's request and have a great adventure in his life based upon what OUR FATHER shares with him. Further, I told him that when we both were done with our great adventures, we would take the time to share with each other what our respective adventures entailed. So I am living my Great Adventure knowing MY FATHER could call me home at any moment. I will get to hear and share our great adventures that we both experienced while we were apart. It will be so much fun to hear what he did and what exciting adventures he had. So I live my greatest life going forward with the hope and vision of being able to share my excitement with my twin.

Prior to doing this exercise, I was always feeling like something was missing in my life. I had spent 30 years searching for "my other half," not knowing why I was doing that. I remember having an *imaginary friend* as a child who I called "brother" and he didn't seem to leave my awareness until I started nursery school. Then it seemed that every year of school, I would latch onto someone who would become my "best friend" for that school year and I would have certain expectations of them and unknowingly put a lot of pressure on that person. It was no wonder every year I would need to find a new best friend. Then when I got into my profession, I transferred all of that energy to my patients and had high expectations of them as well. And when they rejected my care or didn't get the results they were looking for, it prompted me to begin taking many different seminars. Perhaps I didn't know enough. Perhaps there was something missing from my care. It was at a Neuro-Emotional Technique Seminar with Dr. Scott Walker that he helped me discover *My Vanishing Twin*. Upon this discovery, things began to make sense and I could now understand why I had been and acted the way I had for all those years. Now I felt I could "fix" my imbalance and be healed. And for the next 14 years I would go from seminar to seminar to seminar having the latest breakthrough technique applied to me in an effort to re-solve my vanishing twin issue. I would have any practitioner I could meet at these seminars "work" on me and my issue. Things would cycle through feeling improvement and moving back to feeling like nothing had changed. Every time I took a new seminar, I felt like resolution was near, and then I would not feel resolved some months later. Finally, I met Dr. Doug Gilbert who helped me Re-Write My Story. And the transformation was so simple and yet so profound. It actually "pissed me off" that my solution was so obvious, yet I could not see what was right there for the picking. While participating in his Re-Write Your Rules Seminar, we came to this exercise and he very matter of factly asked me how long I had been "working" on my issue and what kind of techniques I have used to help it. When I shared the amount of time and the number of techniques I had spent "working" on my issue, he acknowledged how great a practitioner I must be to have all those tools to help others with. He then asked the perfect question. He asked me *the* question which made my whole world change in an instant. *"What if you simply chose to be done with that issue?"* My world literally stopped. My brain froze and within a millisecond, my mind opened up to a whole new awareness. Was it true that all I needed to do was choose to be done with my story? Could it be that simple? Of course my answer was a very loud YES! And so that night, I went back to my hotel room and I Re-Wrote My Story.

As someone who has done the exercise and shared this story with everyone who has taken my *Quantum Leap© Seminar*, I can assure you that my previous life of being a victim and always feeling rejected by others and always blaming people for not living up to my expectations has vanished. By taking responsibility and telling my new story of encouraging him to leave, rather than feeling *"less than"* or *"not good enough"* because he had *"rejected"* me (an old core belief system that did not serve me in my past relationships), I am now able to relax in the company of others and know that my life is a reflection of what I put out. I am able to engage life without feeling *less than* or *not good enough*. I no longer carry an Un-conscious feeling of being rejected by others. I am able to embrace life and create the types of relationships I choose that are based in my heart's desire.

Now that you understand the purpose behind *Re-writing Your History*, I invite you to do the following exercise for your own clarification. Exercise # 8 is truly transformational. Read through the information that follows and take advantage of the power of this exercise. You will be happy you did.

Exercise # 8
Re-writing Your History

This exercise is useful when you become aware that you are living/telling the same story over and over again.

Neville says with your imagination exercises, you can imagine a new history for yourself; a new start. Remember, what you BELIEVE about your history up to now is what will create your focus for NOW. If you grew up poor, this will likely affect your current relationship with money. To change this, imagine a new childhood for yourself, YOUR childhood, where your parents had (have) plenty of money for what they required and desired. Imagine yourself having all the love you desired and required throughout your childhood.

One effective way to get into your *"new view"* of your life is to revise your memory of your history. I am not talking about changing who your parents were. Notice in the first example I didn't say imagine yourself having grown up rich. No, I said imagine having all your requirements met. There is a big difference between the two. This takes merely a shift in consciousness. The more *"real"* you can imagine it, the more it will change your Un-conscious beliefs, which will in turn, change your focus. The less you *"change"* in your physical history, the more your Un-conscious will *"buy into"* your changes. Small shifts can produce huge changes in consciousness - therefore huge changes in your focus, resulting in huge changes in your outcomes.

This is really about you taking authority in your life...your whole life including your childhood. Having your authority in your life means taking *"authorship"* over your experiences. Notice the root word *"author."* An author is someone who writes what they choose to write. As author of your life, you write your life which you choose to have. The more you write your life, the more you will consciously manifest, create and attract the experiences YOU choose from moment to moment to moment. You can rewrite your past experiences to reflect your new mode of consciousness. You shift your focus. You can do this only in your mind, or journaling as a way to create a new *"script"* for yourself. Remember, for this to have benefits for you, you MUST have authority in your life.

As you do this, begin to come from a place of love. Then by developing the highest form of love, which is compassion for another, this will allow you to let go of your attachment to people showing up for you in a particular way and allow you to take back your power. It allows you to become your own highest authority as you begin to author your life going forward.

Do This For Yourself:
- Think back to an unpleasant memory you have from birth to ten years old. Not a horrible memory or tragic one, just an unpleasant one (it is usually better to start with something manageable and then revise bigger "stuff" after you are well-practiced and confident with this exercise). Now put yourself in your experience of the event while in your full authority to create your experience.
- Identify any other players involved (family, friends, etc), and remember what their roles were.

- What were you thinking and feeling at the time? What is the conscious creative emotion returning to you (see your *Energy of Emotion* chart pg. **31**) during this event?

- Next, remember why you created this situation for yourself a.k.a. what did you get out of the experience? What did you learn from it? What was your benefit of this experience?

- Now shift your focus from the *limiting feelings* around your situation to what your *strength returning* from the situation is. Imagine yourself fully conscious of your strength while you are experiencing the event and now rewrite the event to reflect your new perspective.

- You may rewrite your history in your mind, or put it down on paper. The latter will usually help make your new perspective feel more real for you. Literally, write a new story of what happened. Read it to yourself over and over again out loud until you convince your Un-conscious mind your new story is "real." This will literally change your life history.

_____

_____

_____

_____

_____

_____

_____

_____

_____

_____

_____

_____

_____

_____

_____

_____

_____

_____

_____

_____

_____

_____

_____

_____

Having learned to activate your imagination and tell a new story while knowing what your heart's desire really is, it is important now to put all of that together and take the time to *Create Your Day*. You should do this every day. It is a powerful way to open yourself up to what is possible. You get to experience yourself as the creator. I promise you, if you take the time to do this with intention, be careful what you put out there, because it will come back to you faster than you can believe.

Toolbox Item # 11
Create Your Day...Everyday!

Use this exercise to help yourself get into your feeling of having the life you choose Today!

This is an exercise modified from Dr. Joeseph Dispenza in the movie, "*What The Bleep Do We Know.*" The language has been upgraded to make it more powerful and conscious. For this exercise, please replace the name "*Divinity*" for whatever name(s) you choose to represent the consciousness which created Your Universe.

I am taking this time to create my day because I affect my Quantum Field,
> *The Ocean of energy I exist in,*
> *The Sea of possibility I choose from.*

If it is truth that you, My Divinity are watching me, and through me,
> *And if it is also true that I am a spiritual being,*

Then show me a sign today,
> *That you paid attention to my possibility I choose to manifest,*
> *And bring it to me in a pleasant and surprising way*
> *To assist me in remembering my true nature.*

Here is where you tell your "*Divinity*" what you are creating, and BE in your outcome without any details on HOW it is to be manifest. Remember; DON'T ask FOR it, DECREE FROM having, doing and being it, and use your feelings to prime your manifestation.

Manifest: Manus = hand, Fest = visible

The word manifest means literally to make visible something which already exists in my hands. This is a very important point. Once we desire something, it ALREADY exists energetically. We do not need to struggle or do anything to make it. All that is required is to ALLOW it to come to us. Allow the energy to settle into physicality. To do this, we simply **Let It In.**

The following story is from a previous graduate of *Quantum Leap©* *Seminar.* This is a story that happened to her right after the seminar when she walked into her house.

A Quarter, A Dime or A Nickel?

Driving home from my last day of attending the *Quantum Leap© Seminar* I was reflecting on the message covered that day about how we create our experiences through what we attract into our lives. And I was thinking I was going to test my manifesting abilities and intentionally attract some money.

Earlier that day during the class, *Doc Rick* told a story about an early experiment he experienced with the *Law of Attraction* where he manifested a quarter. He shared that when he began the process he struggled with the decision of which coin he would attempt to manifest. He wanted to go for the quarter but doubted himself and wondered whether a smaller amount, like a penny, might be an easier achievement. What was nice for him was in the end, he got both and as he had asked, it came in a new and surprising way. I contemplated this same thing, which amount would be the most believable to me? A quarter, a dime or a nickel? I had the feeling that they all seemed equally believable and decided that it would work no matter which one I chose. As usual I felt that I needed to prepare for this "monumental task," so I thought that I would set aside some time during the next day or so to make a definite decision on my coin preference and state my intention to manifest it.

I've always thought that there was a very specific formula to manifestation in which the main ingredient was diligence in holding vigil against any thought or emotion that may attempt to sneak in and put the kibosh on the whole thing. Needless to say, in the past with this type of thinking, intentional manifestation was always a difficult task for me and not something I looked to with much excitement or hope of success. It always felt like more of a struggle and most of the time I was defeated.

I began to feel pressure that this process would get in my way and once again ruin my plans. As I reached my home my mind began to shift to more mundane topics and I wasn't at all expecting what happened next. As I walked into my home and began to step over the threshold into the kitchen, there on the floor right where I was about to put my foot, they were, all of three of them, the quarter, the dime and the nickel! I was surprised to say the least at how this "just happened!" I didn't do anything, no ritual, no vigilance against intruding thoughts aimed at the demise of my desire!

The only thing I had done was state my intention and felt that it could happen; I just believed it was possible and then went on with my life.

This lesson for me is twofold: Not only am I creating more experiences of joy in my life, I am more aware of and grateful for those blessings when they happen for me.

Thanks Dr. Rick for helping me to experience this.

As I said at the beginning of this exercise, your results can show up faster than you can imagine. Set your intention, open your heart to your possibility and let go of your expectations that your outcome will show up in a particular fashion. By letting go of the outcome and allowing yourself to simply experience your desired result, without attempting to control the specifics of your desire, you begin to *"let it in."*

The Art of "Letting It In"

Often, we find ourselves up against our own life's resistance. We feel we are being stopped by our life in one way or another, and we notice it doesn't feel very good. This uncomfortable feeling over time will ultimately lead to body dysfunction. It is in this bodily dysfunction that we have hindered our natural well being; the well being that is always flowing to us. This is the reason that we are inspired to reach for a better feeling experience.

So, if we are choosing to find ways to allow the natural feeling of well being to flow, and to flow to us, then we need to find ways to allow our asking, which is more pointed than ever before, to be answered. If you have negative emotion, and you keep focusing as you do, the *Law of Attraction* just keeps bringing more of that negative feeling to you. Likewise, the thoughts keep getting bigger and bigger, as does your emotion. This ultimately results in your physical experience. If you continue the pattern and do nothing about releasing your resistance, or finding a thought that feels better, then it just continues to get even bigger. After all, a disease is or an illness is only a physical indicator, just like the negative emotion was at the beginning. Most people are taught to tolerate or endure negative emotion. Phrases like, "*No one said life was fair; no one said it was going to be fun; buck up and keep a stiff upper lip; big boys don't cry*", and others like them are examples. You've trained yourself to put up with negative emotion as if that was a natural way to live. What I am encouraging you to do is to waken that negative emotion within and recognize it as an indicator of your resistance. Once you '*re-cognize*' - the act or process of knowing again - you've re-contextualized the negative emotion to be a pre-cursor to moving in a positive direction. So, when you feel negative emotion, know that it is pointing at some negative resistance. This is a good thing to become aware of. It is directing you pointedly at something you are consciously aware of that you do not feel positive about. In the middle of the negative emotion and experience, if you are conscious enough of your experience and aware of your negative feeling, stop and ask yourself; "***What is it that is missing here, what is it that I am desiring in this moment? What is it that I am really reaching for? What is at the root of this feeling of frustration (or other emotion)? What is it that I am seeing that I do not choose and that I am pushing against, but am not really pushing away, and instead I'm including in my experience? What is causing me to stop my natural well being from flowing to me? What is causing me to hold my cork, that would naturally float, under the water?***" You are now poised to change this awareness into something positive. What will always happen, and usually pretty quickly is an **awareness** of what is wanted is now being born within that moment. **Clarity** about what is desired comes to mind. Then as you turn more towards what is wanted and softly start talking about that, very often you begin to shift your energy just a little bit, and with this shift, now positive thoughts begin to form in your awareness. Next, your energy begins shifting in a positive direction. Life begins to move in a positive direction. If you continue with those positive thoughts, your environment will begin to change for the better. It all comes down to what you choose to focus on; in what direction - positive or negative - do you choose to focus?

Another way to approach this is by saying, "***I'm going to reach for the thought that feels better.***" Appreciate that you don't always have access to all those great feeling thoughts. You may have to take it in steps to move your way up the scale from the negative emotion to one that feels better. In other words, you can't go from feeling depressed to feeling happy in one simple step. You don't have access to the range to do that. But you do have access to the range within you that enables you to reach for the initial feeling you can grasp for within a smaller range. Then from there, you can find a new feeling that feels better from this new vantage point and reach for the next one within range. In other words, you have to move from **Depression →Anger → Blame→ Frustration → Hopefulness**, before you can even begin to consider feeling **Happy**. Reach for the best thought you have access to in that moment and then focus there for a few seconds or minutes, allowing that new feeling to become the center of your range, before reaching for the next best feeling (refer to the **Emotional Scale©** Chart pg. 32). By focusing yourself there, and becoming stable or grounded in that thought or feeling, the **Law of Attraction** will then allow another thought or feeling to come join with it. Then you can reach for the next thought that feels better from your new, better feeling vantage point. Allow that to become your new center and then allow other thoughts to join with it. Do this repeatedly as you move on up the scale. Soon the original thought, which didn't feel good to you, is out of your range of awareness.

Appreciate that what you think about and what you feel, sets up your frequency of vibration. This frequency resonates throughout your whole body and within every cell. If you are holding a particular thought or feeling for too long, or chronically for short periods of time throughout your life, the cells are going to begin to vibrate at that frequency all the time. If you are flying through life feeling blissful and happy all the time, your cells are going to resonate those feelings and the **Law of Attraction** will give you those kinds of resonant experiences. Likewise, if you are holding a negative emotion in your body and experience that negative emotion regularly, your cells will begin to resonate with the negative energy and soon you will experience life aligned with your negative energy. Your physical body will begin to take on the negative energetic manifestation in its physicality. Your health imbalance will show up. Does that make sense? When a person presents with a particular disease, can you see the way into it, and more importantly, can you feel the way out of it?

The way you get out of this particular situation is to "*simply get out of the way.*" You allow your cells to call in their well-being that naturally is coming their way all the time. You simply allow for it and **Let It In!**

I said in that last paragraph the way you get out of this particular situation is to simply get out of the way. Initially it will not be that simple. That is why I am offering the next piece of information. When you practice what's next over time and become really good at it, and when it becomes your natural state of being, it will then become "*simply get out of the way.*" So pay attention to what comes next and take the time to practice this in your daily life. And before you know it, it will become as simple as I make it sound.

4 Steps To *Letting It In*

1. Set Your Vibrational Tone

Setting Your Vibrational Tone

Your vibrational tone is your point of attraction. Therefore, setting your vibrational tone requires you to take the time to FOCUS 100 % of your thoughts (both conscious and Un-conscious) on a particular feeling or emotion. (See the **Emotional Scale©** for examples) By holding your thoughts and feelings that resonate highest on the chart for your **current state** in your vibrational awareness, and slowly reaching for better thoughts and feelings one or two steps further up the scale, you will allow yourself to move to a better place of thinking and feeling.

2. NO Justifications as to Why

Justifications Derail You

When you begin to come up with reasons *Why* you want to create a particular feeling, emotion or manifestation, the fact that you are justifying your reason why will instantly return you into the vibration of what you don't want. It brings your focus back to a place of lacking. This stops the flow of energy in the direction of positive outcomes. Therefore, never give a reason or justify your choice. Simply focus on your desired outcome and be there now.

3. <u>Appreciation</u>

Appreciation

Appreciation means recognition of the quality, value, significance or magnitude of people and things; a judgment or opinion - especially a favorable one; an expression of gratitude; a rise in value or price - especially over time; awareness or delicate perception - especially of aesthetic qualities or values. To come from a place of appreciation allows for the energy to flow. Appreciation is necessary to manifestation. It opens your heart to positive energy and initiates receiving. Appreciate your outcome and how good it feels to have the desire manifest.

4. <u>Thank You for assisting my focus</u>

Gratitude

Gratitude is a state of being grateful and having thankfulness. This is another aspect of expressing without stopping the flow of energy. Being in the flow of allowing will enable you to experience outcomes faster than you can imagine. Coming from the feeling that it is already true is the final piece of the puzzle. Acting as if it is already true has more pulling power than anything you can do. The Universe will rush to make your vision match your reality.

Understand that things will not change immediately. There is a time delay related to our ability to manifest. It is the 17 second law.

The 17 Second Law

<u>THE TIME DELAY:</u> the time between your thought and the manifestation of that particular thought in physical reality is a bi-product of your ability to offer **pure positive emotion** and hold onto that thought and emotion for a minimum of 17 seconds. Each successive 17 seconds will sponsor another positive thought that goes

with the original, and will be the equivalent of many thousands of hours of physical creating. Holding the focused positive thought and feelings for 68 seconds (4 X 17 seconds) should allow you to begin to see physical changes in your environment. This is how manifestation works. Then continue to nurture the physical changes you see to the level you choose.

Please realize that this will take some practice and some patience. The practice supports strengthening your "muscles of positive thoughts and feelings" and your ability to hold your positive thoughts and feelings for the full 17 seconds. As you release and replace your negative core beliefs with new and upgraded positive beliefs as outlined in this book, you will begin to get stronger and it will become easier and easier as you continue to practice the holding your pure positive emotion for each successive 17 seconds. Have fun with the exercising and strengthening while finding new and exciting positive things to focus on and manifest.

ToolBox Item # 12
Chakras/Desires/Outcomes

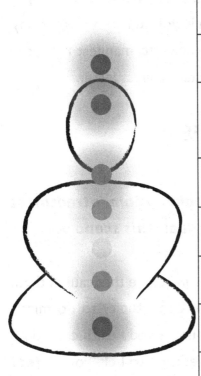

TransPersonal	I Enjoy	Connection To Divine Self
Crown	I Create	I AM Creator
Third Eye	I Love	Recognize I AM Love/ Connected to All
Throat	I Have	Authority and Authorship
Heart	I Choose	Use Love Rather Than Force
Self	I Will	Beginning To Have
Second	I Can	Beginning To Do
Root	I Am	Foundation/Base

Exercise # 9
Chakra Balancing and Meditation

When sitting in a quiet space, center yourself by beginning to belly breathe and quieting your mind. After breathing for several breaths, begin by focusing your attention to your Root Chakra and say the appropriate 2 words associated with it (I Am). Continue focusing energy there for 5 seconds. As you focus your energy on each Chakra, say the appropriate 2 words (i.e. I Am, I Can, etc.) associated with each Energy Center, continuing to focus energy there for 5 seconds. Then move to the next

Energy Center and repeat until you reach the Transpersonal Chakra. Once you have reached your Transpersonal Chakra, continue to sit quietly focusing on your breathing and begin allowing different impressions to surface. Any negative impressions simply thank them and release them. If you become aware of positive impressions, see if you can stay with each until you can ground it in each of your Energy Centers or Chakras. You do this by focusing the energy of each Energy Center or Chakra with the positive impression. Once you have done this for all your Energy Centers, you will have grounded the energy of that positive impression in your energetic light body. Then, when you choose, you can recall that energy and begin to manifest it in your life. Repeating this process every day will make the results manifest faster.

Health and Wellbeing

A Dilemma: Being a deliberate creator in the face of taking/doing a treatment _you do not agree with_, _and how would you approach this scenario?_

Many people today have found themselves in a life circumstance that causes them to "*need*" medication. Possibly they have been given the opportunity to do minor or major "*elective*" surgery (all surgery is elective) for an unwanted health condition. If you find you are using your treatment(s) or you use medicine to help you to **feel better**; allow yourself to feel better. If you find your treatments to be a negative or a burden to you, then you will limit your treatments ability to help you. Do not choose to feel uncomfortable about benefiting from the medicine you use to help you get to a place of **feeling better. Feeling better** is the place you consciously choose to go to if you are truly going to heal. Realize that creation does not mean, "*I have to do everything myself.*" Creation sometimes is a co-creative process.

Confront the fact that you find yourself in a place where you need the help of a treatment/medicine/surgery to assist you in getting to a place of feeling better. Is that acceptable to you? I understand you have found yourself in a place of being out of balance. Out of balance with you and out of balance with what you would consciously choose for yourself. So what if you got out of balance? So what if you didn't know about energy and how it works? So what if you were like most people and you were saying "yes" to some things and "no" to others? So What? So what if you develop some habits of wanting and some habits of pushing against or resisting; so what? So what if you got your energy out of balance which caused this temporary state of being in your physical body, So what? Realize for a moment that each place you stand, each condition or circumstance you become aware of, each of them causes you to have a new desire or thought about **what you would now choose to create,** based upon your new and current perspective. By being in your current state of disease or discomfort, you are creating a newer, stronger desire for wellness then you ever had before. You are more well (in your future) now as a result of this pre-sent disease, than you ever were before the disease began to manifest. The disease is focusing you in a direction you wouldn't have focused had you not had the unwanted condition to begin with. Your desire for a more concrete outcome, a stronger focus if you will, is sponsored by the condition that you are temporarily experiencing through the manifestation of your previous levels of focus/reality and awareness. Does that make sense? The power of your desire is so much greater <u>now</u> and so more clear and focused <u>now</u>, as a result of this temporary condition. Do you feel the pulling power that is within your current temporary condition? Do you feel the incredible pull towards wellness? Can you feel the strong urgency within you to reach for wellness? Do you currently choose to move in the direction of your desire for wellness? That is the pulling power I speak of here. That is the strong desire you have for a state of being that is different from your current temporary state. Remember; all states are temporary at best.

Now what you can choose to do is understand that the pulling power is there, and *the Law of Attraction* is in play. Your next highest outcome is simply to relax, let go and come back to center where you can **let the goodness in**. Let the well-being in. Let the continuous flow of well being into your physical body so it can manifest in your reality. You can do this by experiencing the well being within you *simply* by focusing on the well being within you. This is your natural state of being, Wellness. Choose not to focus on the disease. Focus on your outcome of choice. Focus on your new desired outcome. And so now you can use your current understanding of what you do choose to focus on, a new desire for better well-being, by focusing on feeling better. Does that make sense?

It's easy to do that some of the time, but the time that it is really hard to do is when you are experiencing your condition or pain and feel a need to take the medication or treatment. I would recommend or strongly encourage you to say to yourself, *"This is (my medication or treatment) technology helping me to feel better and to be in balance in terms of my physical body. This is a bridge from my undesired state of being to my new chosen state of wellness. I appreciate what it is doing for me."* Because you are now in a state of appreciation, you are letting your well-being in. You are coming back into balance. Understand that you cannot **appreciate** the energy of well-being and **resist** the energy of well-being from occurring at the same time. They are two opposite energies. Likewise, one cannot love and worry about someone at the same time.

So, consider this. As you are appreciating the effect of your treatment (medicine), appreciating the doctors and scientists who developed the treatment; as you are appreciating the fact that you can bring your body into balance; as you are appreciating feeling better than you once were; as you are appreciating that sometimes you are feeling really, really good; I would encourage you to approach taking your treatment in that way. I would encourage you to use words like *"temporary,"* or say things like, *"This is helping me feel better, and for that I am grateful,"* or *"I'm glad I have you when I need you,"* or other statements like that. In that way, the resistance to your well being will continue to get softer and softer and softer. Once you begin to let the well being in, you begin to experience the well being that you have been so focused on. You will create that wellness and health that you consciously choose for yourself. Do you get that?

Now what is important to understand is that all negative health conditions are created based on the focus on negative energy and outcomes. Perhaps not continuous focus all the time, but even a little at a time for a long period of time will create negative health experiences. So the important question then becomes, **"What's been bothering you?"** What are you worrying about? What are you pushing against, or resisting? From this place, you want to trust that the medication (treatment) is bringing you into balance and let that be a non-issue for a while. In other words, you will deal with all of that later, but for now it is bringing you into balance. You are feeling better as a result. This is important for now.

Now choose to make a new choice that you are going to explore **just a little bit** to see if you can figure out **what it is that is causing the resistance within you to begin with?** Technically you don't have to figure that out, because you could just get happy and go about your business, and in that joyful experience you are smiling and feeling good and healthy, energetic and alive, and because you are holding yourself in that state of allowance, you really don't have to go back and figure out what has been bothering you at all.

However - there is a high degree of likelihood that whatever has been bothering you will have triggered points along the way that will cause you to think about it from time to time. So if you are paying attention to the way you feel, and you feel a flash of negative emotion coming over you, (in other words, you catch yourself becoming aware of the negative circumstance that causes the negative emotions) it's a good time to stop in the middle of that negative emotion and say, *"Oh, this is good, my Internal Guidance System is showing me right now that I have a habit of pushing against and resisting this situation or circumstance. That is part of the reason for holding myself in resistance to the wellness that would naturally be there otherwise, and this is a little piece of the imbalance that is within me."* And now you ask yourself, *"What is it that I am wanting?"* Whenever you are noticing what you do not want, you can then choose what you do want. This will allow you to soften your resistance to, and allow yourself to bridge that energy towards what you do choose. Do you get that? Now you need to consider, **What kinds of things in your experience give you negative emotion,** aside from your health condition? What kinds of things were bothering you pretty regularly before your condition developed? What was your main issue that was so hard to deal with that it made you feel negative emotion? **<u>You want to look apart from the condition of your physical body.</u>** The physical condition developed as a result of your focusing or experiencing negative emotion related to some kind of circumstance or situation in your life. What could those circumstances have been or are they still? The condition of your physical body is always a symptom of something else. Just like a negative emotion is an indication of contradicted energy. Appreciate that the disease is just an exaggeration of that contradicted energy. So it really isn't something to deal with. It will go away when you figure out what the vibration is that is disallowing your well being; when you figure out what you are focused on that causes resistance. It is not that you are not doing things to attract well being. You are naturally attracting well-being. It is that you are doing **more** things that are not allowing your well-being in that you are currently attracting. You know when you are doing those things because you are experiencing negative emotion and symptoms at the same time. So the question to be asking yourself is, ***"What kinds of things come to mind first and loudest and give me negative emotion?"*** If you can, think back before the disease condition developed. Think back before the diagnosis was given. What was the pattern that you experienced or continue to experience today, that causes you negative emotion that you can consciously identify? What is it that you care about so much that isn't occurring in your experience? What feels so hard to overcome? What is it that creates energetic contradiction within you? What is that situation or circumstance that was there before the diagnosis? Are there any circumstances where someone in your life is asking you to do something you do not want to do? Is someone giving you answers that you have not asked for? Is someone causing you to do things you do not want to do? Are any of those *"some ones"* **you** specifically? **In other words, are <u>you</u> causing yourself to do things you do not want to do, in order to keep your job, to stay in relationship, to pay your bills, to live where you live and have the life-style you have? How do you experience justifying your choices in life?** This, more than likely, will be the real reason for your symptom or pain that has manifested in your physical condition. This is what really needs to be addressed in order to let go of the condition and allow your natural well being into your experience. This is what it takes to be a deliberate creator of your health and well being.

This brings us to your final exercise. It is titled "*What Am I Agreeing To In My Life?*" I ask you to consider strongly the following exercise and be honest with yourself. You've moved through this book and found pieces of yourself along the way; you've identified limiting language and other limitations you've enforced upon yourself. You've taken the time to transform some of them and you have more to go, I'm sure. You've taken responsibility and begun being accountable for everything in your life. So take the time to look at this last exercise and remember to be honest with yourself and to give 125 %.

Exercise # 10
What Am I Agreeing To In My Life

Answer the following questions by writing about each question until you realize your justifications for each.

What am I agreeing to in my life in order to keep my life in its current "stable state?"

- Is it something within myself?
- Is it something within my relationship?
- Is it something within my job?
- Is it something within my life-style?

What situation(s) am I holding onto and allowing myself to continue being associated with because letting go of that situation would invite greater difficulty? In other words, what are you holding onto (a fear of something if you let go), that you do not want, but will continue to hold onto because to let go of it would invite something even more difficult to deal with, i.e. less money, being alone, less security, etc. Which one of those fears sponsors your "*need*" to stay associated with the circumstance(s) that brings you the most angst in your life?

Spend some time with this exercise. This is an opportunity for you to really identify and handle any 'excuses' you have allowed for yourself which have hindered your life and stopped you from moving forward. This is your opportunity to change that once and for all, and to allow you to experience yourself as the true creator of your life. Can you feel the power in that? Can you feel the power within you?

Finally I have a concept for you to embrace. And after you have read through the concept, I would strongly urge you to embrace and then put into place this concept. It's called

Say YES to Your Life

I want you to consider what would happen in your life if you embraced; said thank you; allowed yourself to experience everything; and simply said YES to all of it. What do you think would happen to your life? Do you think it would improve? I can guarantee it would improve. I will tell you why that is true, and how in the following pages.

Before I get into that, I have to set the background with some understanding. We have talked about *the Law of Attraction*. It is a three step process. Ask, your Universe responds, receive. Sounds simple enough, Yes? Furthermore it is defined as, *that which is likened to itself is drawn.* You draw to you everything you think and most important, everything you *feel*. In fact, your feelings are your true attractor. You are a magnet; attracting to you through your thoughts, words and deeds. Each is based on your feelings and emotions that sponsor your thoughts. The more you hold your feelings and emotions constant, the more you will think your reality into being. Positive or negative, the results will speak for what your thoughts and feelings are and have been. If you don't like the outcomes/results of your present life, you'll need to change your thoughts and feelings. Change your thoughts and feelings, and you will change your life.

Now, to simply change your thoughts and feelings in this now moment in an effort to make your life go forward is not as easy as it sounds. This is because of your *re-active* mind which is influenced by all of your previous experiences stored in your Un-conscious mind. This currently controls what you see in your outer world and affects how you re-act to it. Furthermore, your current belief system influences your re-active mind and was hard-wired into your Un-conscious mind before you knew enough to say otherwise. You were programmed to believe everything that is possible or not possible from all of your teachers (parents, mentors, relatives, siblings, and others) by the time you were age 6 or 7. If your life is less than ideal and you choose to change it, you could spend a life-time doing therapy and/or going to different seminars and/or reading self-help books and/or trying any of the other methods available to you. Handled that way, the process could potentially take a life-time, and the results still wouldn't be guaranteed. We continue to Un-consciously repeat habit patterns as a natural reaction to what we know to be true, even if it is only *our* truth. This repetition is what keeps us stuck and stops our lives from moving forward at a preferred pace. Most would choose to experience their desired outcomes now. So how can one do that? How does one get to experience their desired outcome sooner, rather than later?

Please go back to the beginning of this chapter - Say YES to Your Life. I want you to consider what would happen in your life if you embraced; said thank you; allowed yourself to experience everything; and simply said YES to all of it. What do you think would happen to your life? Do you think it would improve?

The word YES is very liberating. It is very freeing and allows for movement towards you and through you. Therefore, say YES to what is currently showing up in your awareness, since it has been attracted to you through the *Law of Attraction* from previous thoughts and intentions. This will allow you to be in agreement with your creations, even if you are not conscious of how you created them. When you are in agreement with your creation, you allow your experience of them to be positive and thus allow for more harmony in your life.

I can hear you thinking, *"But what if what has come into my experience is not such a nice thing to experience?"* Well that brings us to the next word requiring clarity, the word *responsibility*. Being responsible means answerable or accountable. The definition continues; *as for something within one's power, control, or management; chargeable with being the author, cause, or occasion of something; having a capacity for moral decisions and therefore accountable; capable of rational thought or action.* Therefore, being responsible for your life requires you to acknowledge **you are the creator of your experience**; this means all of what you experience, both the pleasant and the unpleasant. Let me explain why this is.

If we can agree *the Law of Attraction* is always at work, is always accurate and is always bringing to you an exact energetic match to that which is your loudest thought, or more accurately your dominant feeling, then appreciate that some of what is coming into your life now is as a result of your previous thoughts and feelings. Your present experience in any moment is always the grand total of, and in alignment with, your past dominant thoughts and feelings; *Always and all ways.* Responsibility means to take ownership **of** and to be accountable **for** what you have created. That means both positive and negative creations. This is a challenging concept for most of us. Most people would say *"I do not want this and I did not ask for this!"* to a negative experience which comes into their awareness. I would offer the response of, *"I agree that you did not consciously choose to have this experience. However, what you are not considering is the negative, Un-conscious aspect of how the Law of Attraction works."* Once more, the law states, *that which is likened to itself is drawn.* It doesn't say I will bring you only positive experiences. Again, both positive and negative components go into your results. A blending of both your positive and negative thoughts and feelings is what you will draw to your awareness and then to your experience. Your present result cannot change, for it was created in your past and your Universe has manifested it in your present. It is because of that relationship with the time delay that most people get hung up. Your outward result causes you to reset your feeling state in *re-action* to what is manifesting in your present moment. It becomes a vicious cycle which seems impossible to overcome.

If we go back to the start of this information a third time, I want you to consider what would happen to your life if you embraced, said thank you and allowed everything you experience and simply said YES to all of it. What do you think would happen to your life? Do you think it would improve?

I repeat; the word YES is very liberating. It is very freeing and allows for movement towards and through you. Therefore, say YES to what is currently showing up in your awareness, since it has been attracted to you through the *Law of Attraction* from previous thoughts and intentions. This will allow you to be in agreement with your creations, even if you are not conscious of how you created them. When you are in agreement with your creation, you allow your experience of them to be positive and thus allow for more harmony in your life. By being in your state of agreement, you will allow all your previous thoughts and feelings to manifest in your experience faster. I hope that makes sense. If you are still confused, please take the time to review what has been given so far in this last section and allow it to expand the way you see things. Take that moment before going forward with what is next. Open yourself up to this new perspective. Owning this point is the key to what comes next; both in what I am sharing with you and what will come to you in your life going forward and how you experience it.

When you say YES, life flows. When you say NO, life stops as the energy of creation stops with it. No from *Dictionary.com* reveals the following definition: *a negative used to express dissent, denial, or refusal, as in response to a question or request; used to emphasize or introduce a negative statement; to reject, refuse approval, or express disapproval of; to express disapproval.* Therefore, when something shows up in your experience and you re-act to it with a *"NO,"* you are causing whatever was being attracted to you to stop its movement by offering the resistance of your NO. In other words, your attention to it in the negative causes it to stop moving and now what you are saying no to becomes fixed in your experience. The more attention you give to it in the negative, the more of that negative experience you will have and will continue to have. Therefore, strongly consider doing just the opposite; say "Yes."

Yes from *Dictionary.com* gives the following definition: *used to express affirmation or assent or to mark the addition of something emphasizing and amplifying a previous statement;* <u>*used to express an emphatic contradiction of a previously negative statement or command;*</u> *to give an affirmative reply to; give assent or approval to.* Based on that definition, if you apply an emphatic contradiction of a previously negative statement or command or outcome and give approval to it, it will thus allow the energy of creation to continue flowing. The flowing in the moment will be based in a *"Yes"* to allow the current negative outcome to begin turning toward a positive. As you stick with your process of feeling positive, you will begin moving your results to the positive. Give it the time to change from negative to positive, as the *Law of Attraction* guarantees it will change.

When you are the creator of your experience, being in a positive state will allow you to begin attracting more positive results and creations. Then seeing and, more importantly, experiencing your results as positive will begin to allow you to feel better. Over time, by continuing to say "Yes," the feeling of joy will begin to dominate your experience. Plus, as you move forward in your life in agreement with what you are experiencing, you will begin to change your overall energetic vibration, therefore allowing *the Law of Attraction* to produce better and more joyous results faster for you. It becomes your *"game."* You will know if you are winning your game when your feeling state of consciousness is that of joy. With joy becoming your dominant state of energy, your attraction factor will then begin to bring to you all you could desire at a faster rate and in a more agreeable fashion. Over time, your joy factor will remain constant as you are continually refining your ideas of what you choose based upon what your response is to your current manifestations. That's why it is so important for you to *get everybody else out of your equation.* They've got their own *"game"* going on; they don't understand your game. Give them a break; stop asking them what they think. *Start paying attention to <u>how you feel</u>.* Joy will be yours immediately, and everything else that you have ever thought would make you happy, will start flowing, seemingly effortlessly, into your experience.

Realize that when you consider others and how they fit into *"your"* game, you may initially resist their reaction to your new way of dealing with your life. They won't like the change you are instituting and will resist your change. This is actually a bi-product of you changing while they remain the same and should be seen as a positive indication of your intention for change. Say YES to that aspect and embrace their resistance. Say Yes to their current actions and re-actions and hold to your commitment to your change. Slowly but surely, they will begin to come around. This will always occur before the experience of your change manifests physically for you. This is where it gets *"challenging."* It is challenging in the sense that you will feel everyone is against you. Initially they will be. They are not asking for change, you are. They will naturally resist it which will test your resolve to creating your change. Are you serious, or are you not? You ability to stand and confront their resistance will determine how committed you are. Recognize that *the challenge to change* your response to your current life manifestations that you created from previous thoughts is the energy of change taking place. Change implies newness. This means newness of what you observe and experience. Therefore, understand that the energy of change will show up with opposites of what you desire *first,* in an effort to create the contextual field (back ground) for your true outcome to show up. In other words, light shines brightest when it is surrounded in the dark. To fully experience the light, there needs to be complete darkness. Darkness is the opposite of the state of light. Therefore to experience the new outcome, your Universe will begin by bringing you the opposite of what you are choosing. As an example, look at a white board meant to write on. The white background allows the colors used to write on it to stand out, similar to the way a black-board allows for the white chalk to show up. You need the background to be the opposite of what you wish to see in order for you to see it. The background must appear first in order for the object of your desire to have the ability to show up in your vision of it. It is the opposite background that helps to define the outcome you desire. Therefore, when you do experience the opposite, say *Yes* to the opposite and see it as the beginning of manifesting your desired outcome. The best part of this process is by saying *Yes*, your desired outcome will come to you faster. If you see the opposite and immediately say, *"NO, I do not want this!"* you have stopped your creative process.

Getting back to *the Law of Attraction*, the second part of the three step process says, *"Your Universe answers."* Your process is not to attempt to control the specifics of how it answers by *expecting* it to show up in a certain way or by a certain time. Your expectations will immediately shift your energy into a place of lack, due to the lack of your manifestation from appearing in the specific way you are expecting. Be aware that for your Universe to answer, it may have to change some other aspects of your life first, before you can experience your desired outcome. That change may initially be uncomfortable for you. This can be a strong indication that you are getting ready to manifest your desired outcome. Continue to focus on the receiving and come from a place of gratitude that your desired outcome is on its way. Know that it is on its way, as it is law. In addition, allowing your change to occur means accepting all your change as part of your process, thus allowing what you desire to manifest faster. If you appreciate your change as part of your process; hold on to your asking; and know in your heart of hearts that you will receive it, then your process becomes less of a challenge and can occur without your resistance. If you say *Yes* to your whole process, then your results will come to you that much faster, because you will have allowed for it and offered without resistance. You will have essentially stopped all of your resistance and simply allowed the natural flow of all things to you in an agreeable fashion. The ones that you focus on and agree to consciously will flow to you faster and faster over time. You will become the conscious creator of your experience.

I hope that makes sense for you and that you will put this information into your life. It is transformational when you *play* with these concepts and inject them into your life consciously. Take the time to set up regular *play* time with this information and have some compassion for yourself as you move up your awareness ladder. I am excited about your opportunity to discover consciously who you are and to direct consciously who you choose to be and how you choose to express yourself fully.

These 5 pages are for you to copy and use for other topics

Topic:_____

Write sentences and words that come to mind for your Topic: (use the example from page 13 for help)

_____

_____

_____

_____

_____

_____

_____

_____

_____

Pick the one you like the least from above and write a paragraph about how you feel

_____

_____

_____

_____

_____

_____

_____

_____

Write your new conscious choice(s) for your life. **UPGRADING Exercise # I**

Exercise # 4
Finding Your Negative Core Beliefs

Personal Activity Sheet Date:__/__/__ **Keep this sheet private. Show it only to supportive people**

What Is A Trigger? (Please read this first)

A trigger is anything that regularly ignites immediate and strong reactions inside you for example: yelling, fighting, hitting, screaming, panic, running, hiding, total surrender, freezing or anything often brings on similar feelings such as extreme anger, rage, confusion, terror, worthlessness, devastation, emotional pain or extreme discomfort.

I. When I Am Triggered...

What kind of comments by others, what specific events or actions, what situations, sounds or tone of voice, what kind of touch, or emotion, what kind of music or even a smell can trigger a reaction like these in you?
Below, describe some of these specific events (example: When Kim blamed me for losing the money.) Avoid general or vague examples such as: When I am blamed for losing things. Include events from throughout your life starting with recent ones and moving backwards in time.
Suggestions: When__said__to me; When __criticized me; When I had to do __ to stop __ getting angry; When __ ignored me; When I was left alone by __; When __(who I love) is in pain; When no one even noticed me___; When __ complimented me about__; When __ yelled at me and lectured me about__; When I had to __ in front of everyone; When __ told me and I didn't understand; When I hear __ playing on the radio; When I smell the aroma of __; When __ was so unfair about;

2. Then I Imagined:

In this column, write what you then imagined about YOU or what you told yourself about YOU. For example I imagined __ that I might get hurt again I knew I wasn't Important; I told myself it was all my fault; that I didn't matter.

These are just some of the thoughts that can '*Hot wire*' straight into your most common reactions.

I. WHEN | >

2. WHEN | >

3. WHEN | >

4. WHEN | >

5. WHEN | >

6. WHEN I (for this one perhaps go back a few relationships) | >

7. WHEN I (for this one perhaps go back to your teen years) | >

8. WHEN I (for this one go back to your earliest memories) | >

Finding Your Negative Core Beliefs

Personal Activity Sheet Date:___/___/___ **Keep this sheet private. Show it only to supportive people**

3. Then I felt...
In this column, write what you then felt:
Examples: Hurt, Sad Pain, Panic, Fear, Alone, Guilt, Shame, Embarrassed, Confused, Frustrated, Angry, Terrified, Devastated, Annoyed, Worthless (These are just some of the feelings that switch on your reactions)

4. This is how I reacted or responded (my reaction patterns)
After you are triggered, what do you do automatically (instantly)? Noticing and naming your triggers and then your repetitive patterns are two of the best clues that in turn help you discover your own negative core beliefs. **Examples**: I got angry and yelled at... I became very quiet and didn't say a word. I started to cry. I said things to __ that I knew would make them go away. I panicked. I told__ what I thought he/she wanted to hear. I got very calm and logical and tried to explain. I tried to control him/her. I criticized (attacked) ____ about his/her faults. I smiled and made a joke about it. I felt cold and started to shake. I hit him. I lied. I got drunk. I tried to think positive thoughts. I 'got even.' I sabotaged everything.

If you like, you can play with these four columns at random or in any order. You might start with this one (column 4) and move back to col. I or begin with col. 3

1.
2.
3.
4.
5.
6.
7.
8.

Review of Material

- Your words are powerful. They can be used to create or destroy. Choose wisely.

- Your words go both ways. They tell you about your internal beliefs. They also can be used, by decreeing, to rewrite your internal beliefs.

- Remember, there are no right and wrong, good and bad words. Some words take you away from your desired outcome. Some bring you towards your desired outcomes and some from your desired outcome as already fulfilled. Choose.

- Pay attention to everything you listen to. What new stories are being written in your Un-conscious Mind?

- Focus your thoughts, feelings and words only on what you Consciously choose to create and attract to you.

- Get SPECIFIC. Specificity creates feelings. Feelings are what attract.

- Your commitment is crucial.

- Year Heart (your Internal Guidance) knows your truth...Listen to it!

- Remember to be grateful for what you do have, and be grateful for your desires being already fulfilled. "I am grateful for my new house!"

- Use one-on-one coaching and personal facilitation with Dr. Rick

- Your imagination is a powerful tool to create feelings to attract your desires to you. This is how the *Law of Attraction* plays.

- Use Outcome/Mind Mapping to identify your hearts true desire.

- Make the last thing you say (or feel before you go to bed) your highest choice so your Universe resonates with your desire being fulfilled. Make the first thing you think about in the morning the same.

- Keep your big dreams, goals, and outcomes to yourself until you require outside assistance. This keeps other people's negative thoughts from squashing your dream.

- Follow your bliss – *Joseph Campbell*

- Consider practicing with any of your supporters on a regular basis. (i.e.: Dr Rick)

Food For Thought...

The translation from the original Aramaic (Matthew 7:7) of *"Ask and It shall be given unto you"* is:

Ask, without hidden motive and be surrounded by your answer.
Be enveloped by what you desire that your gladness be full.

Perhaps they knew *The Secret.* i.e. Ask for what you REALLY desire, deep in your heart, then imagine it as already fulfilled in all your senses. Speak only from your desire already fulfilled and your gladness will be full.

I have come to the frightening conclusion.
I am the decisive element in the classroom.
It is my personal approach that creates the climate.
It is my daily mood that makes the weather...
Hiam Ginott

Consider This

We are in the midst of change. It's unavoidable. I receive phone calls and e-mails on a daily basis now from many who are dealing with increased life stress and the anxiety associated with it. I think this is true for all of us to some degree at least. With all that is going on in our lives right now, consider the following information before going forward in your life.

Look at what you have been through in order to get here. It wasn't always easy, right? Even without any of the tools you have now, you were still able to get through. So I ask you this, "*What makes you think tomorrow is going to be any different?*"

We see the real issue is not *whether* you are going to survive, but *how*. Will you be happy, or will you be sad? Will you be excited again about life, or will you be discouraged, disgruntled and disappointed? Will you be a blessing to all whose lives you touch, or will you be a burden to everyone around you?

The way you hold your present experience is the way you create your next. This is why changing your perspective about your future change is so powerful.

The trick now is to transform your *insight* into your *foresight*. The trick is to know this about your tomorrow, *today*. The trick is to be very clear - <u>life is on your side</u>.

Change is coming to you in your future. Your change is change you place in your future with your thoughts, words and actions of Today. These are your <u>Three Tools</u>

of Creation: Your thoughts, Your words, and Your actions. Choose each wisely and go forth in confidence while creating the future you choose to experience.

In Gratitude

I give much credit to Dr. Doug Gilbert who helped inspire me to initially begin teaching *Quantum Leap© Seminar*, and then choosing to put it into the book format you now hold. I did this to help more people discover themselves in a faster way. There was a time where I was discussing with Dr. Doug about taking over his original class, *Re-Write Your Rules* Seminar. Much of my manual's format for *Quantum Leap© Seminar* is based on his information. After strongly considering what we had discussed, I chose to develop the material from my perspective and present our combined data my way. I have changed some of his material to suit my perspective and added quite a bit of my own original information. Although I have compiled quite a bit of information from my life experience and other sources mentioned, I honor Dr. Doug because he showed up in my life when I was searching for guidance to crystallize my years of thoughts and experience into my *Quantum Leap© Seminar* and this manual. Thank You Dr. Doug for your beingness and for your genuine friendship. I am eternally grateful for all you have shared with me.

As I teach this seminar going forward I anticipate my own clarity increasing and additions to the material will naturally occur. I have already had insights into a second seminar designed to take this information and apply it to 9 different aspects of life. These include: *Career, Education, Ethics, Family, Financial, Health, Home, Recreation* and *Spiritual.* I believe that when each student has sufficiently mastered the tools and exercises of *Quantum Leap©*, there will be a natural progression for each to focus specifically on those aspects of life chosen that will transport them to the highest level deemed possible. Coming to your own understanding of which of the 9 is/are most important for your continued growth will be part of that natural progression. I welcome the opportunity to walk with you again as we co-create our conscious world we each dream possible.

Thank You for your Beingness and for being a part of my creative process.
In Gratitude;
Doc Rick

References

This page will always be under construction, because like all of us, I am constantly learning new information from countless different sources, all of which are I.

Gregg Braden, *The Divine Matrix; The Spontaneous Healing of Belief*

Rhonda Byrne, *The Secret*

Hale Dwoskins, *The Sedona Method*

Dr. Wayne Dyer, *The Power of Intention*

Dr. Doug Gilbert, *Re-Write Your Rules Seminar*

Dr. George Goodheart, *Applied Kinesiology Seminars*

Dr. David R. Hawkins, *Power vs. Force*

Esther and Jerry Hicks, *Ask and It Is Given; The Law of Attraction; The Astonishing Power of Emotions*

Bruce Lipton, Ph.D, *The Biology of Belief*

John Nutting, *Growing Awareness* www.growingaware.com

Steve Pavlina, *Personal Development for Smart People*

James Redfield, *The Celestine Prophecy; The Celestine Prophecy-The Movie*

Robert Tennyson Stevens, *Conscious Language: The Logos of Control; Sacred Body Language Translations, Understanding Your Body's Unspoken Language*

Eckhart Tolle, *The Power of NOW, Stillness Speaks, The New Earth*

Dr. Scott and Deb Walker of NET, Inc. and all the seminars I took under their guidance.

Neale Donald Walsch, *Conversations with GOD* (all his books under that title) and everything else he has written, along with several live seminars.

Other Opportunities

If you choose to apply this work at the next highest level while discovering for yourself the next grandest version of the greatest vision you ever held about Who You Are, please feel free to contact me the following ways:

Dr. Richard A. Huntoon
320 Robinson Avenue
Newburgh, New York 12550
(845)561-BACK (2225)

www.spineboy.com

docrick@spineboy.com

As mentioned, I also teach this information in a 2 day hands on seminar called *Quantum Leap© Seminar*. For information regarding my next seminar, please call or e-mail me directly.

What Others Are Saying about Quantum Leap© Seminar

"This is a life changing experience. It helps you to understand just how powerful your thoughts and words can be in changing your life for the better in manifesting your dreams." - Jean D.

"It changed my life in a matter of hours in a major way for the better." -Melissa H.

"Why are you not moving forward - still in pain? He can help you find your core issue that have been stopping you." -Margaret C.

"This will work if they open themselves up to the teachings." -Sam F.

"A Heart-Felt Experience!" -Cynthia R.

"It provides you with more perspectives and techniques to improve and become more aware of yourself." -Bill B.

"I realize that you can only help someone who wants help. When those people are there, my light will be shining and guiding them to also enjoy this class and change their life." - Sandra G.

"I can transform areas of my life in which I have been stuck. I am happier and that will make my life better." -Mary P.

"By making you more conscious, it will enhance your life experiences." -Marta F.

"If you want to open up your life, become at peace with yourself and move forward in your life, come and learn the tools." -Peg A.

"I would highly recommend the course." - Pete M.

"This seminar will give you tools to use to create the life you desire - and give you an opportunity to set aside the time and begin to put those tools to use." - Mary Z.

"It helped me become more aware of the words I use. It helped me to trust my heart again! It helped me re-discover what love is! It helped me eliminate my negative thinking and helped me focus on the outcomes I desire." -Wanda A.

"It is transformational!" -Sonia S.

"You can understand your Negative Core Beliefs, and then you can Transform them!" -Jeff N.

"Get your life back! Thank You Sooo much Dr. Rick for being you! Thank you for making this available and providing such wonderful care for me and your patients! You are an Angel!" - Annie K.

"It is a class with a lot of tools that you can use to help you grow." - Phil T.

"How this knowing will allow you to open up doors in your life you didn't think possible. And Clarity, It's totally empowering. Thank You for choosing me!" - Mia M.

"I would pursue it. Here is an opportunity to gain access to 12 tools from which to draw so you can work on your "stuff" Yourself! You are empowered because you are facilitating yourself."
-Loretta E.

"You will know yourself -- you will have the tools to take the leap of your life." -Renee' S.

"Get started, you can't afford not to do this seminar! You will feel so much better!"
- Michael C.

"The concepts are so simple; the application is fascinating and enlightening. I highly recommend it!" -Jessica Z.

"Do you like how you feel right now? Take this course and you will!" -Deborah C.

Also available is Dr. Huntoon's first book, **When Your Health Matters: *Using Your Body's Natural Rhythms To Restore Your Health*.** This book is 252 pages - a year's worth of healthful information designed to tap into your body's natural rhythms to restore your health one month at a time. Broken down into 12 months, depending on what month of the year it is, you open to the appropriate section and begin applying the information to your life. After a full 12 months, you repeat the process by applying what you have learned the first time through at a deeper level. This book is available through the office or through LuLu.com.

Consciously Yours

Doc Rick